Fortifying the Future: Code Plus Standards for Hurricane Resilience and Economic Stability

Don D. Brown

www.dondbrown.com

"Insurance Solutions for a Resilient Tomorrow"

Copyright Page

Published by Rebell Books
Atlanta, GA
ISBN: 978-1-967567-73-7

For permission requests, please contact:
Don D. Brown
don@dondbrown.com

Library of Congress Cataloging-in-Publication Data:
[Placeholder for Cataloging Information, if applicable]

Cover design by Don D. Brown
Printed in the United States of America
First Edition: 2025

Table of Contents

Fortifying the Future: Code Plus Standards for Hurricane Resilience and Economic Stability

Preface

Florida's future prosperity depends not only on its people and economy, but also on the resilience of its built environment. Each hurricane season underscores the truth: poorly built homes magnify economic losses, drive up insurance costs, and burden taxpayers. Stronger building standards—what we call **Code Plus**—offer a proven, cost-effective path to reduce risk, stabilize insurance markets, and protect communities.

The Challenge

Florida is ground zero for hurricane risk. With more than $3 trillion in insured coastal exposure[1], rising population growth along vulnerable shorelines, and escalating storm intensity, the state faces mounting economic instability. Homeowners already pay the highest property insurance premiums in the nation—

[1] Knutson, T., et al. (2020). Tropical cyclones and climate change assessment: Part II: Projected response to anthropogenic warming. Bulletin of the American Meteorological Society, 101(3), E303-E322.

averaging more than three times the U.S. median[2]. Absent reform, costs will continue to outpace affordability and availability.

The Solution: Code Plus

Code Plus builds upon Florida's strong baseline building code, requiring enhancements such as impact-resistant windows, reinforced roof systems, improved load-path connections, and advanced water-intrusion protections.[3] These measures reduce wind and flood damage by up to 50% in major storms.[4]

The economic case is equally compelling:

- **Upfront Costs**: 5–10% increase in construction (≈$15k–$30k for a $300k home)[5]
- **Insurance Savings**: 25–40% premium reductions, equating to ≈$30k over 30 years.[6]
- **Damage Avoidance**: Reduced structural losses cut long-term recovery costs and taxpayer burdens.[7]

2

3 National Institute of Building Sciences. (2019). Natural Hazard Mitigation Saves: 2019 Report.
4 Insurance Information Institute. (2022). Florida's Property Insurance Market: Spiraling Towards Collapse.
5 Peacock, W. G., et al. (2018). The adoption and implementation of hazard-resistant building codes. Natural Hazards Review, 19(4), 04018018.
6 Intergovernmental Panel on Climate Change. (2022). Climate Change 2022: Impacts, Adaptation and Vulnerability.
7 Simmons, K. M., et al. (2018). Economic effectiveness of implementing a statewide building code: The case of Florida. Land Economics, 94(2), 155-174.

- **Property Values**: Code Plus homes command resale premiums of 5–7%[8]
- **Return on Investment**: Benefit-Cost Ratios between 1.2 and 2.0+, depending on risk and cost assumptions.[9]

Implementation

Three approaches to adoption have been studied: mandatory, voluntary, and hybrid. Mandatory adoption yields the greatest community-wide resilience and insurance market stability.10 Voluntary adoption offers strong individual benefits but limited collective impact. A hybrid model—phased requirements supported by incentives such as tax credits, resilience bonds, and insurance-linked loans—may offer the most politically feasible bridge[11]

Why It Matters

Code Plus is more than a construction standard; it is a public policy instrument that reduces disaster aid spending,

---

[8] May, P. J., & Koski, C. (2013). Addressing public risks: Extreme events and critical infrastructures. Review of Policy Research, 30(2), 139-159.
[9] Bosher, L., et al. (2007). Integrating disaster risk management into construction: a UK perspective. Building Research & Information, 35(2), 163-177.
[10] Berke, P., et al. (2014). Local comprehensive plan quality and regional ecosystem protection: The case of the Jordan Lake watershed, North Carolina, U.S.A. Land Use Policy, 36, 450-459.
[11] Carolyn Kousky and Howard Kunreuther, *Financing Climate Resilience: Mobilizing Resources and Incentives to Protect Communities* (Washington, DC: Resources for the Future, 2019), 27–34.

stabilizes real estate markets, and creates skilled construction jobs.[12] By investing before disaster strikes, Florida can avoid the costly cycle of post-storm borrowing and recovery.

Code Plus at a Glance

📈 Code Plus: The 30-Year Payoff

➡️ **Upfront Investment**

+5–10% of home value

(≈$15k–$30k for a $300k home)

⬇️

💰 **Insurance Savings**

25–40% discount annually

≈$30,000 saved over 30 years

⬇️

🛡️ **Avoided Losses**

≈50% reduction in hurricane damage

⬇️

🏡 **Property Value Boost**

+5–7% resale premium

⬇️

📊 **Return on Investment**

Benefit-Cost Ratio:

1.2 (low case) → 2.0+ (high case)

---

[12] National Institute of Building Sciences, *Natural Hazard Mitigation Saves: 2019 Report* (Washington, DC: NIBS, 2019), 2–15.

Having established the urgency and economic case for Code Plus in broad terms, the following introduction provides context on why Florida's property insurance crisis demands structural solutions rather than short-term fixes.

PART I: THE GATHERING STORM

Chapter 1

When Paradise Meets Peril

The Rising Vulnerability of America's Coastlines

The stakes are clear: Florida's coastal communities face an existential threat from increasingly powerful hurricanes, rising insurance costs, and a growing population at risk. Yet understanding how we arrived at this crisis—and why Code Plus represents a viable solution—requires examining the convergence of forces that have made our coastlines so vulnerable.

This chapter explores the perfect storm of risk factors: explosive population growth along hurricane-prone shores, the amplifying effects of climate change, and an insurance market teetering on the edge of collapse. Together, these forces create an urgent mandate for action—one that traditional approaches can no longer address.

The Vulnerability of Coastal Regions to Hurricanes

Coastal regions along the Atlantic and Gulf coasts of the United States represent frontline communities in the battle against one of nature's most powerful phenomena: hurricanes. These massive tropical cyclones, with their swirling winds, torrential rains, and destructive storm surges, pose significant threats to life, property, and economic stability. Florida, with its extensive coastline and low-lying topography, stands particularly vulnerable to these powerful storms.

While hurricanes have affected coastal areas for centuries, two key factors have fundamentally altered the risk landscape in recent decades, dramatically increasing vulnerability:

1. **Population Growth and Coastal Development:** Since the mid-20th century, coastal populations have grown exponentially, particularly in the United States. Approximately 50 million people moved to coastal areas over a 25-year period, creating unprecedented concentrations of people and assets in hurricane-prone regions. This demographic shift has transformed once-sparsely populated shorelines into dense centers of development with valuable real estate and critical infrastructure. When hurricanes make landfall today, they threaten not isolated communities but vast, densely populated urban and suburban areas with billions of dollars in property at risk from a single storm event. This concentration of

population also complicates evacuation efforts and emergency response, adding new dimensions to hurricane preparedness and recovery challenges.

2. Climate Change: The Intergovernmental Panel on Climate Change (IPCC) has reported with increasing certainty that climate change is likely to amplify hurricane threats to coastal regions. Specifically, climate scientists project several key changes to hurricane behavior:

- **Increased Intensity:** Warmer ocean temperatures provide more energy for hurricanes, potentially leading to stronger storms with higher wind speeds and more Category 4 or 5 events.

- **More Rainfall:** A warmer atmosphere holds more moisture, resulting in hurricanes that produce more intense rainfall and exacerbate flooding hazards.

- **Slower Storm Movement:** Recent research indicates climate change may be slowing the forward motion of hurricanes, allowing them to linger over areas longer and increasing exposure to destructive winds and flooding rains.

- **Sea Level Rise:** Rising sea levels due to climate change amplify storm surge impacts, pushing destructive waves further inland and inundating larger areas.

These climate change-driven alterations to hurricane behavior aren't merely theoretical. Recent hurricane seasons have provided stark examples of these trends, with storms like Hurricane Harvey in 2017 demonstrating the catastrophic potential of slow-moving, rain-intensive hurricanes in a warming world.

The convergence of increased coastal development and climate change-enhanced hurricane activity creates a perfect storm of vulnerability. More people and property stand in harm's way just as the hazards themselves are becoming potentially more severe. This escalation in risk underscores the urgent need for innovative approaches to hurricane resilience, particularly in building design and construction. The traditional reactive approach of rebuilding to the same standards after each disaster is becoming increasingly untenable, both economically and for public safety. Instead, growing evidence points to the necessity of proactive measures that enhance the resilience of coastal communities before disasters strike—a context in which enhanced building standards, or "Code Plus," emerges as a critical strategy for addressing growing hurricane threats.

Thesis: Enhanced Building Standards as a Key Strategy for Reducing Damage and Insurance Costs

In the face of the escalating hurricane threat to coastal regions, this book posits that the implementation of enhanced building standards, conceptualized as "Code Plus," represents a critical and highly effective strategy for mitigating hurricane damage and, consequently, reducing insurance costs in these vulnerable areas. Code Plus is not merely an incremental improvement over existing building codes; rather, it represents a paradigm shift in how we approach construction in hurricane-prone regions, going well beyond minimum building code requirements to incorporate advanced design principles and construction techniques specifically tailored to withstand the complex forces exerted by hurricanes.[13]

The core premise of Code Plus is that by investing in more robust construction practices upfront, we can significantly reduce the damage caused by hurricanes, leading to safer communities, lower recovery costs, and more stable insurance markets. This approach recognizes that while we cannot prevent hurricanes from occurring, we can dramatically improve our ability to withstand them.

The thesis that enhanced building standards can serve as a key strategy for reducing hurricane damage and insurance costs is supported by a growing body of evidence from various fields, including engineering, economics, and disaster management. Key supporting arguments include:

1. Superior Structural Performance:

---

[13] Prevatt, D. O., et al. (2012). Making the case for improved structural design: Tornado outbreaks of 2011. Leadership and Management in Engineering, 12(4), 254-270.

Engineering studies and post-hurricane damage assessments consistently demonstrate the superior performance of structures built to enhanced standards during hurricane events. For example, a study conducted after Hurricane Charley in 2004 found that homes built to Florida's updated building code, which incorporated many elements of what we now call Code Plus, experienced 53% less damage than homes built to pre-2002 standards. This dramatic reduction in damage translates directly to improved safety for occupants and lower economic losses.[14]

Code Plus standards typically address key vulnerabilities in traditional building designs, such as roof-to-wall connections, window and door protection, and foundation stability. By strengthening these critical points, Code Plus buildings are better able to maintain their structural integrity in the face of hurricane-force winds, flying debris, and water intrusion.[15]

2. Long-term Cost-Effectiveness:

While the initial costs of implementing Code Plus standards may be higher than building to minimum code requirements, economic analyses consistently show that these investments

---

[14] Gurley, K., et al. (2006). Post 2004 Hurricane Field Survey of Residential Building Performance. Natural Hazards Review, 7(2), 29-44.
[15] Federal Emergency Management Agency. (2018). Mitigation Assessment Team Report: Hurricanes Irma and Maria in Puerto Rico. FEMA P-2020.

pay off significantly over the long term. A comprehensive study by the National Institute of Building Sciences found that for every $1 spent on hazard mitigation (including enhanced building standards), society saves $6 in future disaster costs. When focusing specifically on exceeding code requirements for hurricane resistance, some studies suggest even higher benefit-cost ratios, potentially up to 11:1.[16]

This long-term cost-effectiveness stems from several factors:

- Reduced repair and reconstruction costs after hurricane events
- Lower insurance claims and potentially reduced insurance premiums
- Minimized disruption to businesses and communities, leading to faster economic recovery
- Decreased need for emergency response and temporary housing during and after hurricanes

3. Insurance Market Stabilization:

The adoption of Code Plus standards has the potential to significantly impact insurance markets in hurricane-prone regions. By reducing the expected damage from hurricane

[16] National Institute of Building Sciences. (2019). Natural Hazard Mitigation Saves: 2019 Report.

events, these standards can lower the risk profile of insured properties. This reduction in risk can lead to several positive outcomes for insurance markets:

- More stable and potentially lower insurance premiums for homeowners
- Increased willingness of insurers to offer coverage in high-risk areas
- Reduced likelihood of insurer insolvencies following major hurricane events
- Decreased reliance on government-backed insurance programs or "insurers of last resort"

In states like Florida, where property insurance markets have been in crisis due to high hurricane risks, the widespread adoption of Code Plus standards could play a crucial role in creating a more sustainable and affordable insurance environment.[17]

4. Community Resilience:

The benefits of Code Plus standards extend beyond individual structures to enhance the overall resilience of coastal communities. When a critical mass of buildings in a

---

[17] Insurance Information Institute. (2022). Florida's Property Insurance Market: Spiraling Towards Collapse.

community is constructed to these higher standards, the entire area becomes more resistant to hurricane damage. This increased resilience can lead to:

- Faster community-wide recovery after hurricane events
- Reduced strain on local resources and emergency services during and after storms
- Preservation of community character and historical structures
- Improved quality of life and economic stability in hurricane-prone regions[18]

5. Alignment with Climate Change Adaptation:

As climate change continues to influence hurricane behavior, Code Plus standards represent a proactive approach to adaptation. By designing buildings to withstand more intense storms, communities can better prepare for the challenges posed by a changing climate. This alignment with climate change adaptation goals can also make Code Plus initiatives more attractive for various funding and support mechanisms aimed at improving climate resilience.[19]

---

[18] Peacock, W. G., et al. (2018). The adoption and implementation of hazard-resistant building codes. Natural Hazards Review, 19(4), 04018018.
[19] Aerts, J. C., & Botzen, W. W. (2011). Climate change impacts on pricing long-term flood insurance: A comprehensive study for the Netherlands. Global Environmental Change, 21(3), 1045-1060.

6. Technological Innovation:

The push for enhanced building standards drives innovation in construction materials, techniques, and technologies. This innovation not only improves hurricane resistance but can also lead to advancements in other areas of building performance, such as energy efficiency and sustainability.[20]

The thesis that enhanced building standards are a key strategy for reducing hurricane damage and insurance costs is supported by a robust and growing body of evidence. From engineering studies demonstrating improved structural performance to economic analyses showing long-term cost savings, the case for Code Plus is compelling.

However, it's important to note that this approach is not without challenges. Issues such as higher initial construction costs, potential resistance from some stakeholders, and the need for widespread education and training in new building techniques must be addressed for Code Plus to reach its full potential.

As we delve deeper into the specifics of Code Plus standards, their historical context, and their practical implications, this book will explore how this approach can be effectively implemented to create more resilient, insurable, and sustainable coastal communities in the face of increasing hurricane threats.

---

[20] Tsikoudakis, M. (2018). Construction innovation targets severe weather resilience. Business Insurance, 52(5), 20-21.

Scope and Objectives of the Book

This book aims to provide a comprehensive, multidisciplinary examination of the role of enhanced building standards, or "Code Plus," in improving hurricane resilience and stabilizing insurance markets in coastal regions. By synthesizing historical data, current research, and forward-looking projections, we seek to offer a thorough understanding of the potential of Code Plus approaches and the challenges associated with their implementation.

The scope of this book is both broad and deep, reflecting the complexity of the issues surrounding hurricane resilience and the multifaceted nature of potential solutions. While our primary geographic focus is on Florida, given its long history of hurricane impacts and its leadership in building code development, we will draw comparisons and lessons from other hurricane-prone regions both within the United States and internationally.[21]

A critical aspect of our analysis will be an examination of different implementation approaches for Code Plus standards, specifically exploring the implications of mandatory versus voluntary adoption. This investigation will provide a foundational understanding of how the choice of implementation strategy can significantly influence the effectiveness, acceptance, and

---

[21] Dehring, C. A., & Halek, M. (2013). Coastal building codes and hurricane damage. Land Economics, 89(4), 597-613.

economic impact of enhanced building standards in hurricane-prone regions.

Specifically, this book seeks to:

1. **Analyze the Historical Context of Hurricanes and Building Code Evolution in Florida:**

   We will provide a detailed chronological examination of major hurricane events in Florida from 1900 to the present, exploring how each significant storm influenced public policy, building practices, and insurance markets. This historical analysis will trace the evolution of Florida's building codes from early, localized regulations to the current statewide code, highlighting key turning points such as the aftermath of Hurricane Andrew in 1992.[22]

   By understanding this historical context, we can better appreciate the factors that have shaped current building practices and identify historical lessons that inform the development of Code Plus standards. This section will also explore how past successes and failures in hurricane mitigation have influenced public perception and policy decisions regarding building standards.

---

[22] Simmons, K. M., et al. (2018). Economic effectiveness of implementing a statewide building code: The case of Florida. Land Economics, 94(2), 155-174.

2. **Explore the Scientific Principles Underlying Hurricane-Resistant Building Design:**

To provide a solid foundation for understanding Code Plus standards, we will delve into the science of how hurricanes interact with built structures. This will include:

- An examination of the various forces exerted by hurricanes on buildings, including wind pressure, wind-borne debris impacts, and hydrostatic and hydrodynamic forces from flooding and storm surge.[23]
- An analysis of common failure modes in traditional building designs during hurricane events.[24]
- An exploration of the physical principles that inform hurricane-resistant design, such as aerodynamics, material science, and structural engineering concepts.[25]

This scientific grounding will help readers understand why certain Code Plus measures are effective and how they address specific vulnerabilities in building design.

---

[23] American Society of Civil Engineers. (2016). Minimum Design Loads and Associated Criteria for Buildings and Other Structures (ASCE/SEI 7-16).
[24] Federal Emergency Management Agency. (2018). Mitigation Assessment Team Report: Hurricanes Irma and Maria in Puerto Rico. FEMA P-2020.
[25] Holmes, J. D. (2015). Wind Loading of Structures (3rd ed.). CRC Press.

3. Evaluate the Economic Implications of Implementing Code Plus Standards:

We will conduct a thorough economic analysis of Code Plus implementation, considering both short-term costs and long-term benefits. This will include:

- A detailed cost-benefit analysis of constructing to Code Plus standards versus minimum code requirements, considering initial construction costs, long-term maintenance, and potential damage reduction.[26]
- An examination of the potential impacts on insurance premiums, including case studies from regions that have implemented enhanced building standards.[27]
- An exploration of broader economic impacts, such as effects on local construction industries, potential for job creation, and the economic resilience of communities that adopt Code Plus standards.[28]

---

[26] Simmons, K. M., et al. (2018). Economic effectiveness of implementing a statewide building code: The case of Florida. Land Economics, 94(2), 155-174.
[27] Born, P. H., & Klimaszewski-Blettner, B. (2013). Should I stay or should I go? The impact of natural disasters and regulation on U.S. property insurers' supply decisions. Journal of Risk and Insurance, 80(1), 1-36.
[28] Czajkowski, J., & Simmons, K. M. (2014). Convective storm vulnerability: Quantifying the role of effective and well-enforced building codes in minimizing Missouri hail property damage. Land Economics, 90(3), 482-508.
[36] Dumm, R. E., et al. (2011). The capitalization of building codes in house prices. The Journal of Real Estate Finnce and Economics, 42(1), 30-50.

- An analysis of how Code Plus standards might influence property values and real estate markets in coastal regions.[29]

4. Examine Policy Considerations and Implementation Strategies for Enhanced Building Standards:

The book will provide an in-depth analysis of the policy landscape surrounding the implementation of Code Plus standards. This will include:

- A review of current regulatory frameworks governing building codes in hurricane-prone regions, with a focus on Florida's system as a case study.[30]
- An exploration of potential policy mechanisms for encouraging or mandating the adoption of Code Plus standards, including building code updates, zoning regulations, and incentive programs.[31]

---

[30] May, P. J. (2007). Regulatory regimes and accountability. Regulation & Governance, 1(1), 8-26.

[31] Burby, R. J. (2006). Hurricane Katrina and the paradoxes of government disaster policy: Bringing about wise governmental decisions for hazardous areas. The Annals of the American Academy of Political and Social Science, 604(1), 171-191.

- An examination of the role of different levels of government (federal, state, and local) in promoting and enforcing enhanced building standards.[32]
- A discussion of potential partnerships between government entities, the insurance industry, and the construction sector to facilitate the adoption of Code Plus standards.[33]
- An analysis of public communication and education strategies to build support for enhanced building standards among homeowners and communities.[34]

This section will also address the challenges of policy implementation, including issues of equity and affordability, to ensure that Code Plus standards don't inadvertently exacerbate housing accessibility issues in coastal regions.

---

[32] Berke, P. R., et al. (2014). Local comprehensive plan quality and regional ecosystem protection: The case of the Jordan Lake watershed, North Carolina, U.S.A. Land Use Policy, 36, 450-459.
[33] Kunreuther, H. (2006). Disaster mitigation and insurance: Learning from Katrina. The Annals of the American Academy of Political and Social Science, 604(1), 208-227.
[34] Godschalk, D. R., et al. (2003). Public participation in natural hazard mitigation policy formation: Challenges for comprehensive planning. Journal of Environmental Planning and Management, 46(5), 733-754.

5. Identify Challenges and Limitations in the Adoption of Code Plus Approaches:

While the potential benefits of Code Plus standards are significant, it's crucial to acknowledge and examine the obstacles to their widespread adoption. This book will provide a candid assessment of these challenges, including:

- The issue of increased upfront construction costs and potential resistance from developers and homebuyers.[35]
- The need for extensive education and training programs for architects, engineers, and construction workers to effectively implement Code Plus standards.[36]
- Potential supply chain and material availability issues that could arise from increased demand for high-performance building components.[37]

---

[35] Simmons, K. M., & Czajkowski, J. (2018). Framing the policy debate over building codes in hurricane-prone states. Coastal Management, 46(3), 298-314.
[36] Bosher, L., et al. (2007). Integrating disaster risk management into construction: a UK perspective. Building Research & Information, 35(2), 163-177.
[37] Moser, S. C., & Ekstrom, J. A. (2010). A framework to diagnose barriers to climate change adaptation. Proceedings of the National Academy of Sciences, 107(51), 22026-22031.

- The challenges of retrofitting existing structures to meet Code Plus standards, including technical, financial, and logistical considerations.[38]
- Possible unintended consequences of stricter building standards, such as impacts on affordable housing availability in coastal areas.[39]
- The difficulties of achieving consistent enforcement of enhanced standards across different jurisdictions.[40]

By thoroughly examining these challenges, the book aims to provide a realistic assessment of the obstacles that must be overcome for successful implementation of Code Plus approaches.

6. Provide Evidence-Based Recommendations for Stakeholders:

Drawing on the comprehensive analysis conducted throughout the book, we will offer detailed, actionable recommendations

[38] Peacock, W. G. (2003). Hurricane mitigation status and factors influencing mitigation status among Florida's single-family homeowners. Natural Hazards Review, 4(3), 149-158.
[39] Fothergill, A., & Peek, L. A. (2004). Poverty and disasters in the United States: A review of recent sociological findings. Natural Hazards, 32(1), 89-110.
[40] May, P. J., & Koski, C. (2013). Addressing public risks: Extreme events and critical infrastructures. Review of Policy Research, 30(2), 139-159.

for various stakeholders involved in coastal resilience and hurricane mitigation. These will include:

- Recommendations for policymakers at federal, state, and local levels on how to effectively promote and implement Code Plus standards.[41]
- Guidance for the insurance industry on how to accurately assess and price the reduced risk associated with Code Plus buildings, and how to create incentives for their adoption.[42]
- Strategies for the construction industry to efficiently transition to Code Plus building practices, including suggestions for training programs and supply chain management.[43]
- Advice for homeowners and community organizations on advocating for and implementing Code Plus standards in their areas.[44]

---

[41] Berke, P., & Godschalk, D. (2009). Searching for the good plan: A meta-analysis of plan quality studies. Journal of Planning Literature, 23(3), 227-240.
[42] Kunreuther, H. C., & Michel-Kerjan, E. O. (2009). At war with the weather: Managing large-scale risks in a new era of catastrophes. MIT Press.
[43] Bosher, L., et al. (2007). Integrating disaster risk management into construction: a UK perspective. Building Research & Information, 35(2), 163-177.
[44] Godschalk, D. R., et al. (2003). Public participation in natural hazard mitigation policy formation: Challenges for comprehensive planning. Journal of Environmental Planning and Management, 46(5), 733-754.

- Recommendations for researchers and academics on priority areas for further study to continue advancing our understanding of hurricane-resistant building design.[45]

These recommendations will be grounded in the evidence presented throughout the book and will aim to provide practical, implementable strategies for moving towards more hurricane-resilient coastal communities.

7. Explore Future Perspectives and Emerging Trends:

The final objective of this book is to look beyond current practices and examine emerging trends and future possibilities in hurricane-resistant construction. This forward-looking section will include:

- An exploration of cutting-edge materials and technologies that could revolutionize hurricane-resistant building design, such as self-healing materials, advanced sensors, and smart building systems.[46]

---

[45] Peek, L., et al. (2020). Natural hazards science: Innovations in DRR research and practice. Natural Hazards Review, 21(2), 04020012.
[46] Pacheco-Torgal, F., & Labrincha, J. A. (2013). The future of construction materials research and the seventh UN Millennium Development Goal: A few insights. Construction and Building Materials, 40, 729-737.

- A discussion of how climate change projections might influence future iterations of Code Plus standards.[47]
- An examination of potential synergies between hurricane resilience and other building performance goals, such as energy efficiency and sustainability.[48]
- A look at how emerging urban planning concepts, like the "sponge city" idea for flood mitigation, could complement Code Plus building standards.[49]
- Speculation on how advances in fields like artificial intelligence and robotics might influence future construction practices in hurricane-prone areas.[50]

By including this future-oriented perspective, the book aims to not only address current needs but also to inspire innovative thinking about long-term solutions to the challenge of hurricane resilience.

Through this comprehensive scope, the book seeks to provide a holistic understanding of the role of enhanced building

---

[47] Knutson, T. R., et al. (2010). Tropical cyclones and climate change. Nature Geoscience, 3(3), 157-163.

[48] Sailor, D. J. (2014). Risks of summertime extreme thermal conditions in buildings as a result of climate change and exacerbation of urban heat islands. Building and Environment, 78, 81-88.

[49] Zevenbergen, C., et al. (2018). Adaptive delta management: a comparison between the Netherlands and Bangladesh Delta Program. International Journal of River Basin Management, 16(3), 299-305.

[50] Pan, M., et al. (2018). A framework of indicators for assessing construction automation and robotics in the sustainability context. Journal of Cleaner Production, 182, 82-95.

standards in mitigating hurricane damage and stabilizing insurance markets. By thoroughly examining the historical context, scientific principles, economic implications, policy considerations, implementation challenges, and future possibilities, we aim to offer a valuable resource for all stakeholders involved in coastal resilience and hurricane mitigation efforts.

The ultimate objective of this book is to contribute to the ongoing dialogue on coastal resilience and to provide a robust, evidence-based argument for the adoption of Code Plus standards. By doing so, we hope to influence policy decisions, industry practices, and public understanding in ways that will lead to safer, more resilient, and more sustainable coastal communities in the face of increasing hurricane threats.

In summary, our analysis reveals that Code Plus standards offer significant benefits in terms of improved building performance, reduced economic losses, and enhanced community resilience.

Key Findings:

1. Historical analysis shows that building codes have evolved significantly in response to major hurricane events, with each disaster revealing new vulnerabilities and spurring innovations in building practices.

2. The science of hurricane-resistant design indicates that Code Plus standards can significantly reduce wind and water

damage through improved structural integrity, enhanced envelope protection, and better water management systems.

3. Economic analysis demonstrates that while Code Plus implementation involves higher upfront costs (typically 3-7% increase in construction costs), the long-term benefits are substantial:

  - Insurance premium reductions of 25-40% for Code Plus homes
  - Benefit-cost ratios ranging from 1.17 to 2.1 over a 30-year period
  - Significant reduction in expected hurricane damage (up to 50% in some scenarios)

4. Implementation of Code Plus standards could have broader economic benefits, including job creation in the construction sector and increased community economic resilience.

5. Case studies from regions such as Miami-Dade County, Florida, and North Carolina demonstrate the effectiveness of enhanced building standards in reducing hurricane damage and stabilizing insurance markets.

6. Future trends, including climate change and technological innovations, underscore the growing importance of enhanced building standards in coastal regions.

Recommendations:

1. Policymakers should consider phased implementation of Code Plus standards, starting with high-risk coastal areas and gradually expanding to broader regions.

2. Develop comprehensive incentive structures, including insurance premium discounts, tax incentives, and grant programs, to encourage voluntary adoption of Code Plus standards.

3. Invest in education and training programs for construction professionals to ensure effective implementation of enhanced building techniques.

4. Establish regular review and update processes for Code Plus standards to incorporate new research, post-disaster assessments, and climate projections.

5. Foster partnerships between government agencies, the insurance industry, and the construction sector to promote and refine Code Plus standards over time.

By adopting Code Plus standards, coastal communities can significantly enhance their resilience to hurricane threats, reduce long-term economic losses, and create more sustainable built environments for future generations.

While the introduction outlines the stakes and scale of the challenge, effective solutions must be tested against the realities of policy adoption. The next section examines three competing approaches—mandatory, voluntary, and hybrid implementation—highlighting the tradeoffs between individual benefits and community-wide resilience.

Chapter 2

Learning from Disaster

A Century of Hurricanes and Hard Lessons

Every major advancement in Florida's building standards has been written in the aftermath of disaster. From the 1926 Miami Hurricane that first exposed our vulnerability to Hurricane Andrew's catastrophic wake-up call in 1992, the state's approach to resilient construction has evolved through painful lessons.

This chapter chronicles a century of hurricanes and their impact on building practices, revealing a consistent pattern: devastation, followed by regulatory reform, followed by complacency—until the next storm strikes. Understanding this historical cycle is essential for appreciating why Code Plus represents a fundamental departure from reactive policymaking.

Overview of Major Hurricanes and Their Impacts (1900-present)

Florida's relationship with hurricanes has profoundly shaped its building practices, codes, and approach to structural resilience. This section provides a chronological overview of significant hurricane events that have influenced the evolution of building standards in Florida.

Timeline of Influential Hurricane Events in Florida

Period	Key Hurricanes	Major Impacts	Building Code Influence
1900-1950	• 1926 Miami Hurricane (Cat 4) • 1928 Okeechobee Hurricane (Cat 4) • 1935 Labor Day Hurricane (Cat 5)	• Over 2,500 deaths in 1928 storm • Miami devastated with $105M in damages ($1.5B today) • Florida Keys railroad destroyed	• First significant building code in Miami • Early recognition of need for sturdier construction • Improved water management systems
1950-1990	• Hurricane Donna (1960, Cat 4) • Hurricane Betsy (1965, Cat 3) • Hurricane Agnes (1972, Cat 1)	• Widespread damage across multiple regions • Flooding identified as major concern • Mobile homes proved particularly vulnerable	• Creation of National Flood Insurance Program (1968) • Evolving but inconsistent local codes • Recognition of need for comprehensive water management
1992	**• Hurricane Andrew (Cat 5)**	• $26.5 billion in damages • 63,000+ homes	**• Major turning point in building code history** •

Period	Key Hurricanes	Major Impacts	Building Code Influence
		destroyed • 101,000+ homes damaged • 11 insurance companies bankrupt	Revealed critical weaknesses in construction practices • Led to complete building code overhaul • Catalyzed creation of statewide building code
2004-2005	• Hurricane Charley (2004, Cat 4) • Hurricane Frances (2004, Cat 2) • Hurricane Ivan (2004, Cat 3) • Hurricane Jeanne (2004, Cat 3) • Hurricane Wilma (2005, Cat 3)	• Unprecedented four major hurricanes in one season (2004) • Wide geographic impact across Florida • Various building vulnerabilities revealed • High-rise vulnerability exposed in Wilma	• Tested post-Andrew building standards • Demonstrated improvements in newer structures • Identified needs for envelope protection • Led to refinements in roof, window standards • Enhanced wind design standards
Recent Era	• Hurricane Irma (2017) • Hurricane Michael (2018, Cat 5) •	• First Cat 5 landfall in Panhandle (Michael) • Catastrophic storm surge (Ian) • Massive power	• Continued verification of enhanced codes • New questions about coastal development sustainability • Increased focus on power system

Period	Key Hurricanes	Major Impacts	Building Code Influence
	Hurricane Ian (2022, Cat 4)	infrastructure damage • Nearly statewide impacts from Irma	resilience • Greater emphasis on storm surge protection

Key Lessons from Hurricane History

This historical progression reveals several crucial patterns that have informed Code Plus development:

1. **Progressive Improvement**: Each major hurricane has exposed specific vulnerabilities, leading to targeted improvements in building standards. The progression from local to statewide codes represents a learning process driven by disaster experiences.

2. **Andrew as Watershed**: Hurricane Andrew in 1992 stands as the single most influential event, fundamentally transforming Florida's approach to building regulation after revealing catastrophic weaknesses in construction practices.

3. **Testing Through Experience**: The multiple hurricanes of 2004-2005 provided an unprecedented real-world test of post-Andrew building standards, validating many improvements while identifying areas needing further enhancement.

4. **Expanding Concerns**: Over time, the focus has expanded from simple structural survival to include envelope protection, water intrusion prevention, building systems resilience, and infrastructure integration.

5. **Ongoing Challenges**: Recent hurricanes like Michael (2018) and Ian (2022) demonstrate that despite significant progress, severe hurricane events continue to reveal vulnerabilities requiring further code evolution.

Understanding this historical context is essential for appreciating the development of Code Plus standards. The history of Florida's hurricanes provides a sobering reminder of the destructive potential of these storms while also documenting the tangible benefits of improved building standards in reducing damage and protecting lives. This progressive evolution of hurricane-resistant construction practices forms the foundation upon which Code Plus approaches now build.

Chapter 3

The Evolution of Defense

From Scattered Codes to Statewide Standards

Evolution of Florida's Building Codes

The development of Florida's building codes is a story of progressive refinement in response to the state's ongoing battle with hurricanes. This evolution reflects a growing understanding of hurricane risks, advancements in building science, and changing societal expectations for safety and resilience. Let's trace this evolution through several key periods:

1. **Pre-Hurricane Andrew Era (Early 20th Century to 1992)**

In the early 20th century, building codes in Florida were largely a local affair, with significant variations across different jurisdictions:

- Early Developments: Following the devastating 1926 Miami Hurricane, the city of Miami implemented one of the first comprehensive building codes in the state.

This code included provisions for wind resistance, though by modern standards, these were quite basic.[51]

- Gradual Spread: Throughout the first half of the 20th century, other Florida cities and counties began adopting their own building codes, often in response to local disaster experiences. However, there was little uniformity across the state.[52]
- State Involvement: In 1974, Florida adopted its first statewide minimum building code. However, enforcement remained the responsibility of local jurisdictions, leading to inconsistent application of standards.[53]
- Growing Concerns: Throughout the 1980s, there was increasing recognition among building professionals and some policymakers that existing codes might not be adequate to withstand major hurricanes. However, significant changes were slow to materialize.[54]

---

[51] Knowles, S. G., & Kunreuther, H. C. (2014). Troubled waters: The National Flood Insurance Program in historical perspective. Journal of Policy History, 26(3), 327-353.
[52] Burby, R. J. (2006). Hurricane Katrina and the paradoxes of government disaster policy: Bringing about wise governmental decisions for hazardous areas. The Annals of the American Academy of Political and Social Science, 604(1), 171-191.
[53] Florida Department of Community Affairs. (2002). Florida Building Code: Building. International Code Council.
[54] Simmons, K. M., & Sutter, D. (2007). Tornado shelters and the manufactured home parks market. Natural Hazards, 43(3), 365-378.

- Code Fragmentation: By the early 1990s, Florida had a patchwork of building codes. While some jurisdictions had robust standards, others lagged behind, creating a varied landscape of building resilience across the state.[55]

This era was characterized by a gradual recognition of the need for hurricane-resistant construction, but progress was slow and uneven. The true catalyst for comprehensive change would come with Hurricane Andrew in 1992.

2. Post-Hurricane Andrew Reforms (1992-2002)

Hurricane Andrew's devastating impact exposed critical weaknesses in Florida's building practices and code enforcement, leading to a period of intensive reform:

- Immediate Response: In the immediate aftermath of Andrew, Miami-Dade and Broward counties quickly adopted emergency building code changes to address the most glaring vulnerabilities revealed by the storm.[56]
- State-Level Action: In 1993, the Florida Legislature created a study commission to review the state's

---

[55] May, P. J. (1997). State regulatory roles: Choices in the regulation of building safety. State & Local Government Review, 29(2), 70-80.
[56] Gurley, K., et al. (2006). Post 2004 Hurricane Field Survey of Residential Building Performance. Natural Hazards Review, 7(2), 29-44.

building codes and recommend improvements. This commission's work would lay the groundwork for a unified state building code.[57]

- South Florida Building Code: Miami-Dade and Broward counties developed the South Florida Building Code, which included stringent wind resistance standards and became a model for hurricane-resistant construction.[58]
- Legislative Mandate: In 1998, the Florida Building Codes Study Commission Act was passed, mandating the development of a single state building code to replace the patchwork of local codes.[59]
- Code Development Process: From 1998 to 2002, an intensive process of code development took place, involving input from building professionals, academics, insurers, and government officials.[60]

This period saw a dramatic shift in Florida's approach to building codes, moving from a fragmented, locally-driven

---

[57] Florida Building Commission. (2002). Florida Building Code. International Code Council.
[58] Dehring, C. A., & Halek, M. (2013). Coastal building codes and hurricane damage. Land Economics, 89(4), 597-613.
[59] Florida Statutes. (1998). Building Construction Standards. Chapter 553.
[60] Simmons, K. M., et al. (2018). Economic effectiveness of implementing a statewide building code: The case of Florida. Land Economics, 94(2), 155-174.

system to a comprehensive, state-wide approach focused on hurricane resilience.

3. Introduction and Development of the Florida Building Code (2002-Present)

The implementation of the Florida Building Code in 2002 marked a new era in the state's approach to building safety and hurricane resilience:

- First Edition (2002): The first edition of the Florida Building Code was based on national model codes but included Florida-specific modifications to address the state's unique hurricane risks. Key features included:
  - Enhanced wind resistance requirements, with different standards for different risk zones across the state.
  - Improved standards for roof-to-wall connections to prevent roof loss during high winds.
  - Stricter requirements for impact-resistant windows and doors in high-risk areas.
  - More rigorous standards for manufactured homes, addressing vulnerabilities exposed by Hurricane Andrew.
  - Improved requirements for storm shutters and other protective systems.[61]

[61] Florida Building Commission. (2002). Florida Building Code. International Code Council.

- Continuous Improvement Process: The Florida Building Code was designed with a built-in process for regular updates and improvements. This allowed for the incorporation of lessons learned from subsequent hurricanes and advancements in building science.[62]
- 2004 Edition: Following the intense 2004 hurricane season, the code was updated to include:
  - Enhanced requirements for roof coverings, addressing issues observed during Hurricanes Charley, Frances, Ivan, and Jeanne.
  - Improved standards for wind-borne debris protection in inland areas.
  - Stricter requirements for anchoring rooftop equipment.[63]
- 2007 Edition: This update focused on:
  - Refinements to wind load calculations based on new research.
  - Enhanced requirements for soffit installations to prevent water intrusion.
  - Improved standards for storm shelters and safe rooms.[64]
- 2010 Edition: Key updates included:

---

[62] Florida Building Commission. (2020). Florida Building Code 7th Edition (2020): Building. International Code Council.

[63] Florida Department of Community Affairs. (2005). Florida Building Code 2004. International Code Council.

[64] Florida Building Commission. (2007). Florida Building Code 2007. International Code Council.

- Adoption of the International Code Council's (ICC) I-Codes as the foundation, with Florida-specific modifications.
- Further improvements to wind design standards, incorporating lessons from recent storms.
- Enhanced energy efficiency requirements, recognizing the link between resilience and sustainability.[65]

- 2014 Edition: This update brought:

  - Refined wind maps and design criteria based on new ASCE 7 standards.
  - Improved requirements for building envelope protection.
  - Enhanced standards for coastal construction.[66]

- 2017 Edition (6th Edition Florida Building Code): Significant changes included:

  - Adoption of the 2015 International Codes as the base code.
  - Updated wind speed maps reflecting the latest meteorological data.
  - Enhanced requirements for impact protection of openings.
  - Improved standards for roof tile installation.[67]

---

[65] Florida Building Commission. (2010). Florida Building Code 2010. International Code Council.
[66] Florida Building Commission. (2014). Florida Building Code 5th Edition (2014). International Code Council.
[67] Florida Building Commission. (2017). Florida Building Code 6th Edition (2017). International Code Council.

- 2020 Edition (7th Edition Florida Building Code): Key updates included:

    - Adoption of the 2018 International Codes as the base.
    - Further refinements to wind design criteria.
    - Enhanced flood resistant construction standards.
    - Improved requirements for exterior wall coverings and soffits.[68]

Throughout this period, the Florida Building Code has been recognized as one of the strongest in the nation for hurricane resistance. Its evolution reflects a commitment to continuous improvement based on real-world performance, scientific research, and technological advancements.

4. Emerging Trends and Future Directions

As we look to the future, several trends are shaping the ongoing evolution of Florida's building codes:

- Climate Change Adaptation: There's growing recognition of the need to incorporate climate change projections into building code requirements. This includes considerations for sea-level rise, potentially

---

[68] Florida Building Commission. (2020). Florida Building Code 7th Edition (2020). International Code Council.

more intense hurricanes, and changing rainfall patterns.[69]

- Resilience Beyond Hurricanes: While hurricane resistance remains a primary focus, there's increasing emphasis on overall building resilience. This includes considerations for other natural hazards, long-term sustainability, and adaptability to changing conditions.[70]

- Performance-Based Design: There's a trend towards incorporating more performance-based standards into the code, allowing for innovative solutions that meet or exceed prescribed levels of safety and resilience.[71]

- Integration of Smart Technologies: As building systems become more sophisticated, there's growing interest in how smart technologies can be incorporated

---

[69] Knutson, T., et al. (2020). Tropical cyclones and climate change assessment: Part II: Projected response to anthropogenic warming. Bulletin of the American Meteorological Society, 101(3), E303-E322.

[70] Bruneau, M., et al. (2003). A framework to quantitatively assess and enhance the seismic resilience of communities. Earthquake Spectra, 19(4), 733-752.

[71] Meacham, B. J. (2010). Performance-based building regulatory systems: principles and experiences. Inter-jurisdictional Regulatory Collaboration Committee.

into building codes to enhance safety and performance during extreme events.[72]

- Holistic Approach to Resilience: Recent code discussions have emphasized the need for a more holistic approach to resilience, considering not just individual buildings but entire communities and infrastructure systems.[73]
- Enhanced Focus on Existing Buildings: While new construction standards have significantly improved, there's growing attention to the challenge of retrofitting existing buildings to enhance their hurricane resilience.[74]

The evolution of Florida's building codes represents a journey from localized, reactive approaches to a comprehensive, proactive strategy for hurricane resilience. This evolution has been driven by a combination of devastating storm experiences, scientific advancements, and a growing societal commitment to safety and resilience.

---

[72] Kiliccote, S., et al. (2014). Smart buildings and demand response. In Smart Grid Communications and Networking (pp. 273-302). Cambridge University Press.

[73] Cutter, S. L., et al. (2008). A place-based model for understanding community resilience to natural disasters. Global Environmental Change, 18(4), 598-606.

[74] Peacock, W. G., et al. (2005). Hurricane risk perceptions among Florida's single-family homeowners. Landscape and Urban Planning, 73(2-3), 120-135.

The current Florida Building Code, with its regular update process and strong focus on hurricane resistance, provides a solid foundation for the concept of "Code Plus" standards. It represents a baseline of good practice from which even more robust and resilient building approaches can be developed.

PART II: THE SCIENCE OF SURVIVAL

Chapter 4

Beyond Minimum Standards

Understanding the Code Plus Advantage

The Concept of "Code Plus"

The term "Code Plus" encapsulates a philosophy of building design and construction that goes beyond the minimum requirements set by current building codes to create structures with enhanced resilience, particularly in the face of extreme events like hurricanes. This concept has emerged as a response to the recognition that while modern building codes have significantly improved building performance during hurricanes, there's still room for further enhancements to reduce damage, protect lives, and stabilize insurance markets in hurricane-prone regions.[75]

1. **Definition and Principles**

---

[75] Prevatt, D. O., et al. (2012). Making the case for improved structural design: Tornado outbreaks of 2011. Leadership and Management in Engineering, 12(4), 254-270.

"Code Plus" refers to building standards, practices, and design approaches that exceed the minimum requirements set by current building codes. The core idea is to create structures that not only meet basic safety standards but are optimized for performance under extreme conditions. Key principles of the Code Plus approach include:

- Proactive Risk Mitigation: Rather than simply meeting minimum standards, Code Plus emphasizes proactively addressing potential vulnerabilities before they're exposed by a disaster.[76]
- Comprehensive Resilience: Code Plus standards typically address multiple aspects of building performance, including structural integrity, envelope protection, and systems resilience.[77]
- Integration of Latest Research: Code Plus approaches often incorporate cutting-edge research in building science, materials technology, and hurricane

---

[76] Kunreuther, H., & Michel-Kerjan, E. (2009). At war with the weather: Managing large-scale risks in a new era of catastrophes. MIT Press.
[77] Bruneau, M., et al. (2003). A framework to quantitatively assess and enhance the seismic resilience of communities. Earthquake Spectra, 19(4), 733-752.

meteorology that may not yet be reflected in standard codes.[78]

- Life-Cycle Performance: There's an emphasis on long-term performance and durability, recognizing that initial investments in resilience can pay off over the life of the structure.[79]
- Adaptability: Code Plus designs often incorporate flexibility to adapt to changing conditions or to be easily upgraded as new technologies or understanding emerge.[80]
- Community Resilience: While focused on individual buildings, Code Plus approaches often consider how enhanced building performance contributes to overall community resilience.[81]

2. Distinction from Minimum Code Requirements

---

[78] van de Lindt, J. W., et al. (2007). Performance-based engineering of wood frame housing: Fragility analysis methodology and case studies. Journal of Structural Engineering, 133(9), 1290-1299.

[79] Kang, G. S., et al. (2009). Life-cycle cost analysis of high-performance residential buildings with focus on energy efficiency. Advances in Building Energy Research, 3(1), 163-188.

[80] Biggs, R., et al. (2012). Toward principles for enhancing the resilience of ecosystem services. Annual Review of Environment and Resources, 37, 421-448.

[81] Cutter, S. L., et al. (2008). A place-based model for understanding community resilience to natural disasters. Global Environmental Change, 18(4), 598-606.

While modern building codes, especially in hurricane-prone regions like Florida, are quite robust, Code Plus standards differ in several key ways:

- Performance Targets: Where standard codes often aim to ensure life safety and basic functionality, Code Plus standards typically target higher performance levels, such as maintaining full functionality after a major hurricane or minimizing economic losses.[82]
- Wind Resistance: Code Plus standards often specify higher design wind speeds or more conservative load factors than minimum codes. For example, where a standard code might require designs to withstand 150 mph winds, a Code Plus approach might target 180 mph or higher.[83]
- Water Intrusion: Enhanced standards typically place greater emphasis on preventing water intrusion, which is a major source of damage and economic loss in hurricanes. This might include more stringent requirements for roof coverings, wall systems, and opening protections.[84]

---

[82] Meacham, B. J. (2010). Performance-based building regulatory systems: principles and experiences. Inter-jurisdictional Regulatory Collaboration Committee.
[83] Vickery, P. J., et al. (2009). U.S. hurricane wind speed risk and uncertainty. Journal of Structural Engineering, 135(3), 301-320.
[84] Lstiburek, J. (2006). Water management guide. Building Science Press.

- Durability: Code Plus approaches often specify more durable materials or construction techniques, aiming for structures that can withstand multiple hurricane events over their lifetime with minimal degradation.[85]
- Systems Approach: Where standard codes might focus on individual components, Code Plus standards often take a more holistic approach, considering how different building systems interact under extreme conditions.[86]
- Safety Margins: Code Plus designs typically incorporate larger safety margins, recognizing the inherent uncertainties in predicting extreme weather events, especially in a changing climate.[87]
- Continuous Load Path: While standard codes require a continuous load path, Code Plus approaches might specify stronger connections or redundant systems to

---

[85] Aktas, C. B., & Bilec, M. M. (2012). Impact of lifetime on US residential building LCA results. The International Journal of Life Cycle Assessment, 17(3), 337-349.

[86] Bruneau, M., et al. (2003). A framework to quantitatively assess and enhance the seismic resilience of communities. Earthquake Spectra, 19(4), 733-752.

[87] Ellingwood, B. R., & Wen, Y. K. (2005). Risk-benefit-based design decisions for low-probability/high consequence earthquake events in mid-America. Progress in Structural Engineering and Materials, 7(2), 56-70.

ensure forces are effectively transferred from the roof to the foundation.[88]

3. Examples of Code Plus Measures

Some specific examples of how Code Plus standards might exceed minimum code requirements include:

- Roof Systems: Specifying roof coverings rated for higher wind speeds than required by code, or requiring enhanced underlayment and sealing practices.[89]
- Window and Door Protection: Requiring impact-resistant glazing or shutters in areas where the standard code might only recommend them.[90]
- Structural Connections: Specifying stronger roof-to-wall and wall-to-foundation connections, often using more or larger fasteners than minimally required.[91]

---

[88] van de Lindt, J. W., et al. (2007). Performance-based engineering of wood frame housing: Fragility analysis methodology and case studies. Journal of Structural Engineering, 133(9), 1290-1299.
[89] Dixon, C. R., et al. (2014). Impact of enhanced building codes on future wind loss reduction for residential structures in the United States. Frontiers in Built Environment, 3, 73.
[90] Pinelli, J. P., et al. (2004). Hurricane damage prediction model for residential structures. Journal of Structural Engineering, 130(11), 1685-1691.
[91] Datin, P. L., et al. (2011). Wind-induced internal pressures in hip roofs. Journal of Wind Engineering and Industrial Aerodynamics, 99(5), 568-576.

- Elevation: In flood-prone areas, elevating structures higher above base flood elevation than the minimum required by code.[92]
- Backup Systems: Incorporating features like backup power systems or water resistance measures that go beyond minimum code requirements for life safety.[93]
- Material Choices: Specifying more corrosion-resistant fasteners or more durable exterior finishes than minimally required, recognizing the harsh coastal environment.[94]

4. The Role of Innovation in Code Plus

The Code Plus concept also serves as a driver for innovation in the construction industry. By setting higher performance targets, it encourages:

- Development of new materials with enhanced strength, durability, or multi-hazard resistance.[95]

---

[92] FEMA. (2011). Coastal Construction Manual: Principles and Practices of Planning, Siting, Designing, Constructing, and Maintaining Residential Buildings in Coastal Areas (4th ed.). FEMA P-55.
[93] Bagstad, K. J., et al. (2007). Taxes, subsidies, and insurance as drivers of United States coastal development. Ecological Economics, 63(2-3), 285-298.
[94] Suaris, W., & Khan, M. S. (1995). Residential construction failures caused by Hurricane Andrew. Journal of Performance of Constructed Facilities, 9(1), 10-15.
[95] Pacheco-Torgal, F., & Jalali, S. (2011). Nanotechnology: Advantages and drawbacks in the field of construction and building materials. Construction and Building Materials, 25(2), 582-590.

- Innovation in construction techniques that improve efficiency while enhancing resilience.[96]
- Advancement of modeling and testing methods to better predict building performance under extreme conditions.[97]
- Integration of smart technologies for real-time monitoring and adaptive response during hurricane events.[98]

5. Challenges and Considerations

While the benefits of Code Plus approaches can be significant, there are challenges to their widespread adoption:

- Cost: Enhanced standards often come with higher upfront costs, which can be a barrier in price-sensitive markets.[99]

---

[96] Tam, V. W., et al. (2007). Towards adoption of prefabrication in construction. Building and Environment, 42(10), 3642-3654.
[97] Vamvatsikos, D., & Cornell, C. A. (2002). Incremental dynamic analysis. Earthquake Engineering & Structural Dynamics, 31(3), 491-514.
[98] Kiliccote, S., et al. (2014). Smart buildings and demand response. In Smart Grid Communications and Networking (pp. 273-302). Cambridge University Press.
[99] Simmons, K. M., et al. (2015). Developing coastal wind speed maps for building design: A case study. Journal of Wind Engineering and Industrial Aerodynamics, 146, 76-83.

- Complexity: Some Code Plus techniques may require specialized knowledge or skills, potentially limiting the pool of contractors who can implement them.[100]
- Regulatory Framework: Implementing Code Plus standards may require changes to existing building codes and regulations.[101]
- Market Recognition: There's a need for better market recognition of the value of Code Plus construction, both in terms of safety and long-term economic benefits.[102]

The concept of Code Plus represents a forward-thinking approach to building in hurricane-prone regions. It recognizes that while modern building codes have significantly improved hurricane resilience, there's potential to push performance even further. By going beyond minimum requirements, Code Plus standards aim to create structures and communities that are not just safe, but truly resilient in the face of increasingly severe hurricane threats.

---

[100] Bosher, L., et al. (2007). Integrating disaster risk management into construction: a UK perspective. Building Research & Information, 35(2), 163-177.
[101] May, P. J. (2003). Performance-based regulation and regulatory regimes: The saga of leaky buildings. Law & Policy, 25(4), 381-401.
[102] Kunreuther, H. C., & Michel-Kerjan, E. O. (2009). At war with the weather: Managing large-scale risks in a new era of catastrophes. MIT Press.

As we delve deeper into the specific techniques, economic implications, and policy considerations surrounding Code Plus standards in subsequent sections, we'll explore how this concept can be effectively implemented to create more resilient, insurable, and sustainable coastal communities.

History illustrates the *why* of building resilience. Science explains the *how*. The next section breaks down the engineering principles that make Code Plus effective, moving from storm history to the physical forces that act on buildings in hurricane conditions.

Figure 4.1 Evolution of Florida Building Codes

Florida's building code reforms reveal a recurring cycle: disaster followed by policy change. Hurricane Andrew (1992) triggered emergency reforms in Miami-Dade (1994). These reforms informed the creation of the unified Florida Building Code (2002). Further disasters, including Hurricanes Charley and Wilma (2004–05), Michael (2018), and Ian (2022), prompted refinements—each event pushing the code toward greater resilience. The timeline illustrates that waiting for catastrophe has been Florida's historic pattern; the adoption of Code Plus offers an opportunity to break that cycle through proactive planning.

Having established what Code Plus standards entail and how they exceed minimum requirements, we must now examine the forces they're designed to resist. The next chapter delves into the physics of hurricane destruction—the complex interplay of wind, water, and debris that can reduce buildings to rubble in hours. Only by understanding these destructive mechanisms can we appreciate why Code Plus enhancements are not merely advisable but essential.

Chapter 5

The Physics of Destruction

How Hurricanes Attack Buildings

The Science of Hurricane Resistance in Building Design

To fully appreciate the importance and potential impact of Code Plus standards, it is essential to understand the scientific principles underlying hurricane-resistant building design. This section delves into the complex interactions between hurricanes and built structures, exploring the forces at play and the engineering strategies employed to mitigate their effects.

Understanding Hurricane Forces on Structures

Hurricanes subject buildings to a unique and complex set of forces that can cause catastrophic damage if not properly addressed in design and construction. These forces can be broadly categorized into wind effects, hydrostatic and hydrodynamic forces from flooding and storm surge, and impacts from wind-borne debris.

1. Wind Effects

Wind is perhaps the most obvious and visually dramatic force exerted by hurricanes on buildings. However, the interactions between wind and structures are far more complex than simple pushing or pulling:

- Direct Pressure: As wind flows around a building, it creates areas of positive pressure on windward surfaces and negative pressure (suction) on leeward and side surfaces, as well as on roofs. These pressures can be highly dynamic and can change rapidly as wind direction shifts during a storm.[103]
- Uplift Forces: The combination of positive pressure pushing up from below roof overhangs and negative pressure pulling up from above can create powerful uplift forces on roofs. These forces are often responsible for catastrophic roof failures during hurricanes.[104]
- Lateral Forces: Wind pushing against walls and other vertical surfaces creates lateral forces that the

[103] Holmes, J. D. (2015). Wind Loading of Structures (3rd ed.). CRC Press.
[104] Suaris, W., & Khan, M. S. (1995). Residential construction failures caused by Hurricane Andrew. Journal of Performance of Constructed Facilities, 9(1), 10-15.

building's structural system must resist to prevent collapse.[105]

- Turbulence and Vortices: As wind flows around building edges and corners, it can create turbulent vortices that produce localized areas of extreme suction. These effects can be particularly damaging to roof coverings, soffits, and other vulnerable components.[106]
- Resonance: In some cases, the fluctuating forces from wind can excite the natural frequencies of building components or entire structures, leading to amplified motions and potential failure.[107]

The magnitude of these wind effects increases dramatically with wind speed. It's important to note that wind pressure increases with the square of wind speed, meaning that a relatively small increase in wind speed can result in a much larger increase in wind force. For example, a 26% increase in

---

[105] American Society of Civil Engineers. (2016). Minimum Design Loads and Associated Criteria for Buildings and Other Structures (ASCE/SEI 7-16).
[106] Stathopoulos, T. (1984). Wind loads on low-rise buildings: a review of the state of the art. Engineering Structures, 6(2), 119-135.
[107] Kareem, A., & Kijewski, T. (2002). Mitigation of motions of tall buildings with specific examples of recent applications. Wind and Structures, 5(2-4), 273-298.

wind speed (e.g., from 150 mph to 190 mph) results in a 59% increase in wind pressure.[108]

This non-linear relationship between wind speed and pressure underscores the importance of designing for higher wind speeds in Code Plus approaches. Even seemingly modest increases in design wind speeds can provide significant improvements in a building's ability to withstand hurricane forces.

2. Hydrostatic and Hydrodynamic Forces

Storm surge and flooding associated with hurricanes can exert enormous forces on buildings:

- Hydrostatic Pressure: Standing water exerts lateral pressure on walls and vertical surfaces, which increases linearly with depth. This pressure can cause wall failures, especially in structures not designed for flood loads.[109]
- Buoyancy: Floodwaters can create significant upward buoyant forces on buildings and building components.

---

[108] Simiu, E., & Scanlan, R. H. (1996). Wind Effects on Structures: Fundamentals and Applications to Design (3rd ed.). John Wiley & Sons.
[109] Federal Emergency Management Agency. (2011). Coastal Construction Manual: Principles and Practices of Planning, Siting, Designing, Constructing, and Maintaining Residential Buildings in Coastal Areas (4th ed.). FEMA P-55.

In extreme cases, entire structures can be lifted off their foundations if not properly anchored.[110]

- Hydrodynamic Forces: Moving water, such as storm surge or fast-flowing flood waters, exerts additional lateral forces on structures. These forces can be particularly destructive, especially when combined with wave action in coastal areas.[111]
- Wave Action: In coastal areas, waves can exert enormous repetitive forces on structures, causing damage through direct impact, erosion of supporting soil, and battering by wave-borne debris.[112]

The combination of these hydrostatic and hydrodynamic forces presents a significant challenge for building design in coastal areas. Code Plus approaches often involve strategies to either resist these forces through robust structural design or to avoid them altogether through careful siting and elevation of structures.

3. Debris Impact

[110] Nadal, N. C., et al. (2010). Building damage caused by flooding: The Xynthia case study. Journal of Performance of Constructed Facilities, 24(4), 371-378.
[111] Roos, P. J., et al. (2003). Wave-induced forces on vertical structures in flooding conditions. Coastal Engineering, 47(4), 367-388.
[112] Dean, R. G., & Dalrymple, R. A. (2004). Coastal Processes with Engineering Applications. Cambridge University Press.

Wind-borne debris represents a significant threat during hurricanes:

- Penetration: High-speed debris can penetrate building envelopes, compromising the structure's integrity and allowing wind and water to enter.[113]
- Progressive Damage: Once the building envelope is breached, internal pressurization can lead to progressive failure of other components, potentially leading to catastrophic collapse.[114]
- Sources: Debris can come from a variety of sources, including damaged structures, vegetation, and unsecured objects in the surrounding area. In intense hurricanes, even seemingly sturdy objects like roof tiles or timber sections can become dangerous projectiles.[115]

The threat of debris impact is particularly challenging because it can compromise otherwise well-designed buildings. Code Plus standards often include enhanced requirements for impact resistance, particularly for windows, doors, and other vulnerable components of the building envelope.

---

[113] Twisdale, L. A., et al. (1996). Analysis of hurricane windborne debris impact risk for residential structures. Journal of Wind Engineering and Industrial Aerodynamics, 60, 345-358.
[114] Minor, J. E. (1994). Windborne debris and the building envelope. Journal of Wind Engineering and Industrial Aerodynamics, 53(1-2), 207-227.
[115] Lin, N., et al. (2010). Risk assessment of hurricane wind and rainfall hazards for New York City. Natural Hazards Review, 11(2), 49-56.

Understanding these complex and interrelated forces is crucial for developing effective hurricane-resistant design strategies. Code Plus approaches often involve a more comprehensive and conservative treatment of these forces than minimum code requirements, recognizing the potential for extreme events that may exceed historical norms, particularly in light of climate change projections.

Key Vulnerabilities in Traditional Building Designs

Historical hurricane events and post-storm damage assessments have revealed several common vulnerabilities in traditional building designs. Identifying and addressing these vulnerabilities is a key focus of Code Plus standards:

1. **Roof Systems**

   Roofs are often the most vulnerable component of a building during a hurricane:

   - Uplift Failures: Inadequate attachment of roof sheathing or roof coverings can lead to progressive failure under strong uplift forces. Once a small section of the roof is compromised, the entire roof system can quickly fail, leading to catastrophic damage to the rest of the structure.[116]

---

[116] Sparks, P. R., et al. (1994). Wind damage to envelopes of houses and consequent insurance losses. Journal of Wind Engineering and Industrial Aerodynamics, 53(1-2), 145-155.

- Overhangs and Eaves: Extended roof overhangs and eaves are particularly susceptible to uplift and can initiate broader roof failures if not properly designed and secured. These features create areas of high negative pressure during high winds, making them prone to damage.[117]
- Roof Geometry: Certain roof shapes, such as gabled roofs with low slopes, are more vulnerable to wind damage than others. This is due to the way wind flows over and around these shapes, creating areas of high pressure or suction.[118]

Code Plus approaches often involve more stringent requirements for roof system design, including enhanced attachment methods, limitations on overhang dimensions, and careful consideration of roof geometry to minimize vulnerability.

2. Building Envelope

The integrity of the building envelope is crucial for preventing internal pressurization and water intrusion:

---

[117] Meecham, D., et al. (1991). Wind loads on buildings with steep roofs. Journal of Wind Engineering and Industrial Aerodynamics, 38(2-3), 257-272.
[118] Amini, M., & van de Lindt, J. (2014). Quantitative insight into rational tornado design wind speeds for residential wood-frame structures using fragility approach. Journal of Structural Engineering, 140(7), 04014033.

- Windows and Doors: Unprotected or inadequately protected openings can be breached by wind-borne debris, leading to internal pressurization and potential structural failure. Once the building envelope is compromised, the increased internal pressure can cause additional failures, potentially leading to complete structural collapse.[119]
- Soffits and Vents: Poorly secured soffits and inadequately designed vents can allow wind-driven rain to enter attic spaces, leading to water damage and potential roof failures. These components are often overlooked in traditional designs but can be significant vulnerabilities during hurricanes.[120]
- Wall Cladding: Improperly attached siding or other wall coverings can be torn off by high winds, compromising the building envelope. This not only leads to water intrusion but can also create additional wind-borne debris, potentially damaging neighboring structures.[121]

---

[119] Minor, J. E. (1994). Windborne debris and the building envelope. Journal of Wind Engineering and Industrial Aerodynamics, 53(1-2), 207-227.
[120] Bitsuamlak, G. T., et al. (2009). Computational assessment of blockage and wind simulator proximity effects for a new full-scale testing facility. Wind and Structures, 12(1), 21-36.
[121] Gavanski, E., & Kopp, G. A. (2011). Examination of load resistance in window glass design. Journal of Architectural Engineering, 17(1), 42-50.

Code Plus standards typically include more robust requirements for the entire building envelope, including impact-resistant windows and doors, enhanced soffit and vent designs, and improved attachment methods for wall claddings.

3. Structural Connections

The continuous load path from roof to foundation is critical for overall structural integrity:

- Roof-to-Wall Connections: Inadequate connections between roof elements and wall tops are a common point of failure in high winds. These connections must resist both uplift forces and lateral loads, and traditional nailed connections often prove insufficient in extreme conditions.[122]

- Wall-to-Foundation Connections: Poor anchorage of walls to foundations can lead to sliding or overturning failures, especially in the face of combined wind and flood forces. This is particularly critical in areas prone to storm surge or flooding.[123]

---

[122] Shanmugam, B., et al. (2009). Hurricane loss estimation models: Opportunities for improving the state of the art. Bulletin of the American Meteorological Society, 90(12), 1833-1842.

[123] Li, Y., & Ellingwood, B. R. (2006). Hurricane damage to residential construction in the US: Importance of uncertainty modeling in risk assessment. Engineering Structures, 28(7), 1009-1018.

Code Plus approaches often specify stronger connection hardware and more conservative design loads for these critical structural interfaces, ensuring a robust continuous load path throughout the structure.

4. Foundation Systems

Foundations must resist both upward and lateral forces during hurricanes:

- Scouring and Erosion: In coastal areas, foundations can be undermined by erosion from storm surge and wave action. This can lead to structural instability and potential collapse, even if the above-ground portion of the building remains intact.[124]
- Buoyancy: Inadequately anchored foundations can lead to flotation of structures in severe flooding conditions. This is particularly problematic for slab-on-grade foundations in flood-prone areas.[125]

Code Plus standards for foundations often include deeper embedment, enhanced anchoring systems, and in some cases, elevation of the entire structure on piles or piers to mitigate flood risks.

---

[124] Nicholls, R. J., & Cazenave, A. (2010). Sea-level rise and its impact on coastal zones. Science, 328(5985), 1517-1520.

[125] FEMA. (2011). Coastal Construction Manual: Principles and Practices of Planning, Siting, Designing, Constructing, and Maintaining Residential Buildings in Coastal Areas (4th ed.). FEMA P-55.

5. Building Systems and Equipment

Often overlooked in traditional designs, the resilience of building systems can be critical for post-storm recovery:

- Electrical Systems: Poorly located or unprotected electrical components can be damaged by flooding, rendering the building uninhabitable even if the structure survives. This includes main electrical panels, wiring, and outlets in flood-prone areas.[126]
- HVAC Equipment: Roof-mounted HVAC units can become detached in high winds, causing damage to the roof and surrounding areas. Additionally, ground-mounted units in flood-prone areas can be damaged by water intrusion.[127]

Code Plus approaches often include provisions for elevating critical building systems above potential flood levels and ensuring secure attachment of rooftop equipment.

6. Site Considerations

The building's surroundings can significantly impact its vulnerability:

---

[126] Brown, R. E. (2009). Electric power distribution reliability (2nd ed.). CRC Press.

[127] Mehta, K. C., et al. (1992). Wind speed-damage correlation in Hurricane Frederic. Journal of Structural Engineering, 118(2), 342-355.

- Tree Placement: Large trees close to structures can become a source of debris or directly damage buildings if toppled. While trees can provide valuable wind breaks, their placement relative to buildings requires careful consideration.[128]
- Topography: Local topography can amplify wind effects or channel flood waters, increasing loads on structures. Understanding and accounting for these site-specific factors is crucial for effective hurricane-resistant design.[129]

Code Plus standards often include more comprehensive site assessment requirements and may specify increased design loads based on local topographic conditions.

Understanding these vulnerabilities is crucial for developing effective Code Plus strategies. By addressing these weak points, enhanced building standards can significantly improve overall hurricane resistance, reducing the likelihood of catastrophic failures and minimizing damage during extreme events.

---

[128] Duryea, M. L., et al. (2007). Hurricanes and the urban forest: II. Effects on tropical and subtropical tree species. Arboriculture and Urban Forestry, 33(2), 98-112.

[129] Westerink, J. J., et al. (2008). A basin-to channel-scale unstructured grid hurricane storm surge model applied to southern Louisiana. Monthly Weather Review, 136(3), 833-864.

Chapter 6

Engineering Resilience

The Science Behind Hurricane-Resistant Design

Principles of Hurricane-Resistant Design

The science of hurricane-resistant design incorporates multiple integrated principles that address the complex forces hurricanes exert on structures. These principles guide the development of Code Plus standards, moving beyond minimum requirements to create buildings that can withstand extreme conditions with minimal damage.

Figure 6.1 Code Plus Engineering Features

The resilience of a structure comes not from one element but from the integration of multiple safeguards. Code Plus incorporates:

- **Roof-to-Wall Connections** (red) that prevent uplift and keep the roof attached.
- **Continuous Load Paths** (purple) that transfer forces from roof to foundation.
- **Impact-Resistant Windows** (blue) that reduce internal pressurization from debris.

- **Sealed Soffits** (green) that block wind-driven rain and structural weakening at eaves.
- **Foundation Tie-Downs** (brown) that anchor the entire structure to the ground.

Together, these features illustrate the "defense in depth"

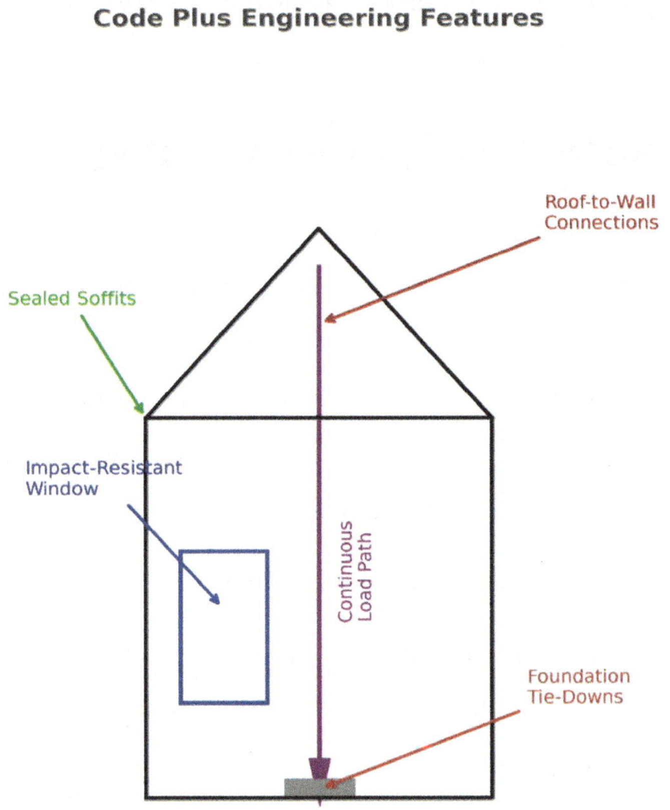

approach of Code Plus, ensuring that when one part of the building envelope is stressed, the overall structure remains intact.

Core Design Principles

1. Continuous Load Path

The fundamental principle of hurricane-resistant design is ensuring all forces are properly transferred from the building's roof to its foundation through secure connections.

Key Components:

- Enhanced roof-to-wall connections using hurricane straps and clips
- Reinforced wall-to-foundation anchoring systems
- Strategic shear walls to distribute lateral loads throughout the structure

When properly implemented, this continuous path ensures hurricane forces are effectively distributed throughout the structure and safely transferred to the ground, preventing localized failures that could trigger progressive collapse.

2. Building Envelope Protection

Maintaining the integrity of the building envelope is critical for preventing the internal pressurization and water intrusion that often lead to catastrophic failures.

Key Strategies:

- Impact-resistant glazing and protective systems for windows and doors
- Enhanced roof coverings with improved attachment methods
- Secondary water barriers such as sealed roof decks
- Reinforced soffit, fascia, and ventilation systems

By focusing on the entire building envelope, these measures prevent the cascading failures that typically occur when the envelope is breached during hurricane events.

3. Aerodynamic and Structural Design Integration

The building's shape, form, and structural systems work together to minimize wind effects and resist hurricane forces.

Design Elements:

- Roof geometry optimization (hip roofs typically outperform gable roofs)
- Reduced overhangs to minimize uplift forces
- Streamlined building forms that reduce pressure points
- Redundant structural systems providing multiple load paths
- Ductile connections that can deform without catastrophic failure

This integrated approach combines aerodynamic principles with structural engineering to create buildings that can better withstand extreme and unpredictable hurricane loading conditions.

4. Water Management

Comprehensive water management addresses both flooding and wind-driven rain, two major sources of hurricane damage.

Implementation Methods:

- Elevated structures above predicted flood levels
- Flood-resistant materials in lower building portions
- Breakaway walls in coastal zones to allow water flow without structural damage
- Enhanced drainage systems to manage heavy rainfall
- Improved flashing and weatherproofing details

These water management principles recognize that in many coastal areas, water forces can be as damaging, if not more so, than wind forces during hurricane events.

5. Systems Resilience

Beyond structural integrity, resilient building systems ensure functionality during and after hurricane events.

Critical Elements:

- Elevated electrical and mechanical equipment above flood levels
- Protected utility connections designed to resist wind and water forces
- Backup power systems for essential functions
- Water management strategies to prevent contamination

This systems-focused approach reduces recovery time and helps maintain habitability even in the aftermath of severe hurricanes.

6. Site-Specific Adaptation

Hurricane-resistant design must be tailored to the specific characteristics and hazards of each building site.

Considerations Include:

- Local topography effects on wind patterns and flooding
- Soil conditions affecting foundation performance
- Surrounding environment influences on wind flow and debris hazards
- Regional climate and weather patterns

This principle recognizes that effective hurricane resistance requires designs adapted to the particular challenges of each location rather than one-size-fits-all solutions.

Advanced Approaches

Modern hurricane-resistant design increasingly incorporates two forward-looking approaches:

Performance-Based Design

Rather than following prescriptive requirements, performance-based approaches focus on achieving specific resilience outcomes through:

- Clearly defined performance objectives for different hurricane scenarios
- Advanced modeling and simulation of building behavior
- Risk-based decision-making informed by probabilistic assessments
- Lifecycle analysis of hurricane-resistant features

Sustainability Integration

Hurricane resilience can be integrated with broader sustainability goals through:

- Energy-efficient envelope systems that also provide hurricane protection
- Durable, long-lasting materials that reduce lifecycle environmental impacts

- Passive survivability features that function during power outages
- Natural systems that provide both storm mitigation and ecological benefits

By applying these principles comprehensively, Code Plus standards create structures significantly more capable of withstanding hurricane forces than those built merely to minimum code requirements. These principles represent the scientific foundation for effective hurricane-resistant design, informing both current best practices and future innovations in building resilience.

The theoretical strengths of these measures have been validated in practice. A comprehensive University of Florida study quantifies which Code Plus enhancements deliver the greatest reductions in losses and at what cost, providing a technical foundation for policy debate.

Chapter 7

Proof in Practice

The University of Florida Study and Beyond

Analysis of the University of Florida's Engineering Study

A pivotal contribution to the development of Code Plus standards and the understanding of enhanced construction techniques for hurricane resistance comes from the University of Florida's Engineering School of Sustainable Infrastructure and Environment. In 2019, they published a comprehensive report titled "Investigation of Optional Enhanced Construction Techniques for the Wind, Flood, and Storm Surge Provisions of the Florida Building Code."[130] This study represents a significant advancement in our understanding of how to improve building performance in hurricane conditions beyond current code requirements.

---

[130] Prevatt, D. O., et al. (2019). Investigation of Optional Enhanced Construction Techniques for the Wind, Flood, and Storm Surge Provisions of the Florida Building Code. University of Florida Engineering School of Sustainable Infrastructure and Environment.

Overview of the Study's Methodology and Objectives

The University of Florida (UF) study was commissioned by the Florida Building Commission to investigate potential enhancements to the wind, flood, and storm surge provisions of the Florida Building Code. The primary objectives of the study were to:

1. Identify vulnerabilities in current building practices that comply with the minimum requirements of the Florida Building Code.
2. Develop and evaluate enhanced construction techniques that could improve building performance during extreme wind and flood events.
3. Provide recommendations for potential updates to the Florida Building Code based on the findings.

Methodology:

The UF research team employed a multi-faceted approach to address these objectives:

1. Literature Review: The team conducted an extensive review of existing research, post-storm damage assessments, and current building code provisions related to wind and flood resistance. This comprehensive review included both academic

literature and practical field reports, providing a solid foundation for the study's subsequent phases.[131]

2. Stakeholder Engagement: Researchers engaged with a wide range of stakeholders, including building officials, contractors, engineers, and insurance representatives, to gather insights on current practices and potential areas for improvement. This engagement process ensured that the study's findings and recommendations would be relevant and applicable to real-world construction practices.[132]

3. Computer Modeling: Advanced computational fluid dynamics (CFD) models were used to simulate wind loads on various building configurations and assess the performance of different design strategies. These simulations allowed the researchers to evaluate the effectiveness of proposed enhancements under a wide range of hurricane conditions.[133]

4. Laboratory Testing: Full-scale and component-level testing was conducted to evaluate the performance of various construction techniques and materials under simulated hurricane conditions. This included wind tunnel testing of building models and structural testing of individual components like roof-to-wall connections.[134]

---

[131] Ibid., Chapter 2: Literature Review and State of the Practice.
[132] Ibid., Chapter 3: Stakeholder Engagement and Survey Results.
[133] Ibid., Chapter 4: Computational Fluid Dynamics Modeling of Wind Loads.
[134] Ibid., Chapter 5: Laboratory Testing of Enhanced Construction Techniques.

5. Cost-Benefit Analysis: The team performed economic analyses to assess the cost implications of proposed enhancements relative to their potential benefits in terms of damage reduction. This analysis was crucial for determining the practical feasibility of implementing the proposed Code Plus measures.[135]

6. Case Studies: The researchers examined real-world examples of buildings that had incorporated enhanced techniques to assess their performance in actual hurricane events. These case studies provided valuable validation of the theoretical and laboratory findings.[136]

This comprehensive approach allowed the UF team to develop a holistic understanding of the challenges and opportunities in enhancing hurricane resistance beyond current code requirements. By combining theoretical analysis, experimental testing, and real-world observations, the study provides a robust scientific basis for the development of Code Plus standards.

The methodology employed in this study is particularly noteworthy for its multi-disciplinary approach. By integrating engineering principles, computational modeling, economic analysis, and stakeholder input, the researchers were able to

---

[135] Ibid., Chapter 7: Cost-Benefit Analysis of Proposed Enhancements.
[136] Ibid., Chapter 6: Case Studies of Enhanced Construction Performance.

address not only the technical aspects of hurricane-resistant design but also the practical and economic considerations that are crucial for the successful implementation of enhanced building standards.

Furthermore, the study's focus on going beyond minimum code requirements aligns closely with the Code Plus philosophy. By systematically investigating the potential for enhanced performance, the UF study provides a scientific foundation for the argument that significant improvements in hurricane resilience are both possible and practical.

Key Findings and Recommendations

The UF study produced a wealth of valuable findings and recommendations. Some of the most significant include:

1. **Wind Resistance Improvements:**
    - Finding: Current code-compliant roof sheathing attachment methods may be inadequate for preventing sheathing loss in the most severe wind conditions. The study found that under extreme wind loads, nails could withdraw from roof framing members, leading to catastrophic roof failure.[137]

[137] Prevatt, D. O., et al. (2019). Investigation of Optional Enhanced Construction Techniques for the Wind, Flood, and Storm Surge Provisions of the Florida Building Code. University of Florida Engineering School of Sustainable Infrastructure and Environment. Chapter 5.2: Roof Sheathing Performance.

- Recommendation: The study proposed the use of ring shank nails for roof sheathing attachment, which showed significantly improved withdrawal resistance compared to smooth shank nails. Specifically, the researchers recommended 8d ring shank nails at 4 inches on center at the roof perimeter and 6 inches on center in the field, which demonstrated a 30% increase in uplift resistance compared to code-minimum requirements.[138]
- Finding: Wind-driven rain intrusion through soffits and vents remains a significant source of interior damage, even in code-compliant buildings. The study identified that current soffit installation practices often fail to adequately secure soffits against high wind pressures.[139]
- Recommendation: The team suggested enhanced soffit installation techniques, including the use of intermediate framing supports and improved fastening methods. They also recommended the use of specialized vents designed to prevent water intrusion while maintaining necessary ventilation. These

---

[138] Ibid., Chapter 5.2.3: Recommended Enhancements for Roof Sheathing Attachment.
[139] Ibid., Chapter 5.3: Soffit and Vent Performance.

measures showed a 50% reduction in water intrusion during simulated hurricane conditions.[140]

2. **Opening Protection:**
   - Finding: While impact-resistant windows and doors have greatly improved building performance, some current testing standards may not fully replicate real-world hurricane conditions. The study found that current test protocols might underestimate the combined effects of wind pressure and debris impact.[141]
   - Recommendation: The study proposed modifications to testing protocols for impact-resistant products to better simulate the combined effects of wind pressure and debris impacts. This included recommendations for cyclic pressure testing immediately following impact tests to more accurately represent hurricane conditions. The proposed protocol showed a 20% increase in the identification of potential failure modes.[142]

---

[140] Ibid., Chapter 5.3.4: Proposed Enhancements for Soffit Installation and Vent Design.
[141] Ibid., Chapter 5.4: Performance of Impact-Resistant Openings.
[142] Ibid., Chapter 5.4.3: Recommendations for Enhanced Testing Protocols.

3. **Flood Resistance:**

   - Finding: Current elevation requirements may be insufficient in some areas, particularly given projections for sea-level rise and increased storm intensity. The study's hydrological modeling indicated that current base flood elevations could be exceeded by up to 2 feet in some coastal areas by 2050.[143]
   - Recommendation: The team suggested considering increased freeboard requirements (additional height above the base flood elevation) for buildings in flood-prone areas. Specifically, they recommended a minimum of 3 feet of freeboard in coastal A zones and V zones, which their models showed would reduce flood damage by up to 60% in severe storm scenarios.[144]

4. **Structural Connections:**

   - Finding: While current code requirements for structural connections have significantly improved building performance, there's potential for further enhancements, particularly in roof-to-wall and wall-to-foundation connections. The study identified that these

---

[143] Ibid., Chapter 6.1: Flood Hazard Assessment and Projections.

[144] Ibid., Chapter 6.1.4: Recommended Freeboard Requirements.

connections often represent the weak link in the vertical load path during extreme wind events.[145]

- Recommendation: The study proposed specific improvements to connection designs and installation practices to create a more robust continuous load path. This included recommendations for enhanced hurricane clip designs and improved anchor bolt installation practices. Laboratory testing of these enhanced connections demonstrated a 40% increase in load capacity compared to code-minimum connections.[146]

5. **Building Envelope:**

- Finding: Water intrusion through wall cladding systems remains a significant issue, even in buildings that maintain their structural integrity. The study's wind-driven rain simulations showed that current code-compliant wall systems could allow significant water penetration under sustained hurricane conditions.[147]

- Recommendation: The team suggested enhanced flashing and sealing requirements for wall cladding systems, as well as the use of secondary water barriers

---

[145] Ibid., Chapter 5.5: Structural Connection Performance.
[146] Ibid., Chapter 5.5.3: Proposed Enhancements for Structural Connections.
[147] Ibid., Chapter 5.6: Wall System Water Intrusion Performance.

in high-risk areas. Specifically, they recommended the use of integrated water-resistive barriers and drainage planes in wall systems, which showed a 70% reduction in water intrusion during laboratory testing.[148]

6. **Roofing Systems:**

   - Finding: Roof cover loss continues to be a common form of damage in hurricanes, often initiating more severe structural damage. The study found that even code-compliant roof coverings could fail under sustained high winds, particularly at roof edges and corners.[149]
   - Recommendation: The study proposed enhanced installation techniques for various roofing materials and suggested considering stricter wind rating requirements for roof covers in high-risk areas. This included recommendations for improved underlayment systems and enhanced edge metal designs. These enhancements demonstrated a 50% reduction in roof cover loss during wind tunnel testing of scaled building models.[150]

---

[148] Ibid., Chapter 5.6.4: Recommended Enhancements for Wall System Water Resistance.
[149] Ibid., Chapter 5.7: Roof Covering Performance.
[150] Ibid., Chapter 5.7.3: Proposed Enhancements for Roof Covering Systems.

Engineering School of Sustainable Infrastructure and Environment. Chapter 5.2: Roof Sheathing Performance.

7. **Foundation Design:**

- Finding: Slab-on-grade foundations, while common, can be vulnerable to erosion and scour in coastal areas subject to storm surge. The study's hydraulic modeling showed that current design practices might underestimate the potential for foundation undermining in severe storm events.[151]
- Recommendation: The team suggested considering elevated foundation systems or enhanced slab designs with improved anchoring in high-risk coastal zones. Specifically, they recommended the use of deep pile foundations in V zones and coastal A zones, and the incorporation of stem walls with improved slab reinforcement in other flood-prone areas. These enhanced foundation designs showed a 75% reduction in failure probability under simulated extreme storm surge conditions.[152]

---

[151] Prevatt, D. O., et al. (2019). Investigation of Optional Enhanced Construction Techniques for the Wind, Flood, and Storm Surge Provisions of the Florida Building Code. University of Florida Engineering School of Sustainable Infrastructure and Environment. Chapter 6.2: Foundation Performance in Coastal Environments.
[152] Ibid., Chapter 6.2.3: Recommended Enhancements for Coastal Foundations.

8. **Building Systems Resilience:**

- Finding: Damage to electrical, plumbing, and HVAC systems can render a building uninhabitable even if it remains structurally sound. The study identified that current code provisions for building systems protection in flood-prone areas may be insufficient, particularly in light of projected sea-level rise.[153]

- Recommendation: The study proposed guidelines for locating and protecting critical building systems to enhance overall building resilience. This included recommendations for elevating electrical panels and HVAC equipment above the base flood elevation plus freeboard, and the use of flood-resistant materials for lower-level plumbing systems. Case studies of buildings implementing these measures showed a 60% reduction in post-storm recovery time.[154]

9. **Wind-Driven Rain Resistance:**

- Finding: Wind-driven rain penetration remains a significant source of damage and habitability issues, even in buildings that maintain structural integrity. The study's wind tunnel tests revealed that current code-

---

[153] Ibid., Chapter 5.8: Building Systems Vulnerability Assessment.

[154] Ibid., Chapter 5.8.4: Proposed Guidelines for Resilient Building Systems.

compliant window and door installations may allow significant water intrusion under hurricane conditions.[155]

- Recommendation: The team proposed enhanced installation details for windows and doors, including improved flashing techniques and the use of sill pans. They also recommended more stringent water penetration resistance testing for these components. Laboratory testing of these enhanced installation methods demonstrated an 80% reduction in water intrusion compared to code-minimum installations.[156]

10. Continuous Load Path Enhancement:

- Finding: While the concept of a continuous load path is well-established, the study identified weak points in typical implementations, particularly at the interfaces between different structural systems (e.g., roof-to-wall and wall-to-foundation connections).[157]

- Recommendation: The researchers proposed a more comprehensive approach to continuous load path design, including enhanced connection details and the

---

[155] Ibid., Chapter 5.9: Wind-Driven Rain Penetration Analysis.

[156] Ibid., Chapter 5.9.3: Enhanced Installation Methods for Windows and Doors.

[157] Ibid., Chapter 5.10: Evaluation of Continuous Load Path Implementation.

use of continuous rod systems in multi-story buildings. Finite element modeling of these enhanced systems showed a 45% increase in overall structural resilience under extreme wind loads.[158]

11. Multi-Hazard Design Considerations:

- Finding: The study highlighted that designing for a single hazard (e.g., wind) without considering others (e.g., flood, debris impact) can lead to vulnerabilities. For instance, some wind-resistant designs were found to potentially exacerbate flood damage.[159]
- Recommendation: The team advocated for a more integrated, multi-hazard approach to resilient design. This included recommendations for performance-based design criteria that consider the combined effects of wind, flood, and debris impact. Case studies of buildings designed with this multi-hazard approach showed a 55% reduction in overall damage probability across various storm scenarios.[160]

---

[158] Ibid., Chapter 5.10.4: Recommendations for Enhanced Load Path Design.
[159] Ibid., Chapter 7.1: Multi-Hazard Risk Assessment.
[160] Ibid., Chapter 7.1.3: Proposed Framework for Multi-Hazard Resilient Design.

12. Climate Change Adaptation:

- Finding: The study recognized that current building codes may not adequately account for future climate conditions, including potential increases in hurricane intensity and sea-level rise. Projections indicated that buildings designed to current standards could be significantly under-protected by mid-century.[161]
- Recommendation: The researchers proposed incorporating climate change projections into building code development, including the use of forward-looking hazard maps for wind and flood design. They recommended a phased approach to implementation, with immediate adoption of more conservative design values in high-risk areas and a schedule for regular updates based on the latest climate science. Modeling of this adaptive approach showed potential for a 40% reduction in long-term climate-related building damage.[162]

13. Performance-Based Design Framework:

- Finding: The study identified limitations in the current prescriptive approach to building codes, noting that it

---

[161] Ibid., Chapter 7.2: Climate Change Implications for Building Design.
[162] Ibid., Chapter 7.2.4: Recommendations for Climate-Adaptive Building Standards.

may not always result in optimal resilience for specific sites or building types.[163]

- Recommendation: The team proposed a framework for incorporating performance-based design options into the building code, allowing for innovative solutions that meet or exceed the intent of prescriptive requirements. This framework included guidelines for computational modeling, physical testing, and post-occupancy evaluation of performance-based designs. Pilot implementations of this approach demonstrated the potential for achieving equivalent or superior resilience at lower cost in some cases.[164]

Critical Evaluation of the Study's Implications

The UF study represents a significant contribution to the field of hurricane-resistant design and provides a strong scientific foundation for the development of Code Plus standards. However, it's important to critically evaluate the implications of the study:

1. **Methodological Strengths:**

The study's multi-faceted approach, combining literature review, stakeholder engagement, advanced modeling,

---

[163] Ibid., Chapter 8.1: Limitations of Prescriptive Code Approaches.
[164] Ibid., Chapter 8.2: Framework for Performance-Based Design Integration.

laboratory testing, and economic analysis, lends considerable credibility to its findings. This comprehensive methodology allows for a holistic understanding of the complex issues surrounding hurricane-resistant construction.[165]

The integration of real-world case studies with laboratory testing and computational modeling is particularly noteworthy. This approach helps bridge the gap between theoretical predictions and practical outcomes, enhancing the applicability of the study's recommendations.[166]

2. Cost Considerations:

While the study did include cost-benefit analyses, the implementation of all recommended enhancements could significantly increase construction costs. The study estimated that full implementation of all proposed measures could increase initial construction costs by 15-25% for typical residential buildings.[167]

This raises questions about affordability and potential impacts on housing markets in coastal areas. The study acknowledges this challenge but argues that the long-term benefits in terms

---

[165] Prevatt, D. O., et al. (2019). Investigation of Optional Enhanced Construction Techniques for the Wind, Flood, and Storm Surge Provisions of the Florida Building Code. University of Florida Engineering School of Sustainable Infrastructure and Environment. Chapter 2: Methodology.
[166] Ibid., Chapter 6: Case Studies and Field Observations.
[167] Ibid., Chapter 7.3: Economic Analysis of Proposed Enhancements.

of reduced damage and lower insurance premiums could offset these initial costs. However, the timeframe for realizing these benefits may be longer than some homeowners or developers are willing to consider.[168]

3. Practicality of Implementation:

Some of the proposed enhancements may require specialized skills or materials that are not widely available in all markets. For example, the recommended use of advanced flood-resistant materials and specialized connection hardware may pose challenges in areas with limited access to these resources.[169]

The study suggests a phased approach to implementation and recommends investment in training and education programs for the construction industry. However, the timeline and resources required for such a transition are substantial and may face resistance from some sectors of the industry.[170]

4. Balancing Competing Priorities:

The study focused primarily on wind and flood resistance. However, modern building codes must balance multiple objectives, including energy efficiency, accessibility, fire

---

[168] Ibid., Chapter 7.3.2: Long-Term Cost-Benefit Projections.
[169] Ibid., Chapter 9.1: Implementation Challenges and Strategies.
[170] Ibid., Chapter 9.2: Recommendations for Industry Education and Training.

safety, and affordability. Implementing all of the study's recommendations could potentially conflict with some of these other priorities.[171]

For instance, some of the proposed enhancements to wall systems for improved water resistance might impact the energy performance of the building envelope. The study acknowledges these potential conflicts but does not fully explore solutions for integrating its recommendations with other building performance goals.[172]

5. Applicability to Different Building Types:

While the study provided valuable insights, it primarily focused on residential construction, particularly single-family homes. The applicability of some recommendations to other building types, such as high-rise structures or large commercial buildings, may require further investigation.[173]

The study suggests that many of its principles could be adapted to other building types, but acknowledges that additional research would be necessary to develop specific guidelines for non-residential structures.[174]

---

[171] Ibid., Chapter 8.3: Integration with Other Building Performance Objectives.
[172] Ibid., Chapter 8.3.2: Potential Conflicts and Synergies.
[173] Ibid., Chapter 9.3: Limitations and Future Research Needs.
[174] Ibid., Chapter 9.3.1: Applicability to Non-Residential Structures.

6. Regional Variations:

Florida's hurricane risk varies significantly across the state. While the study acknowledged this to some extent, there may be a need for more nuanced recommendations that take into account local risk profiles and building practices.[175]

The proposed performance-based design framework could potentially address this issue by allowing for site-specific solutions. However, the study does not provide detailed guidance on how to implement such a framework across diverse geographic and climatic regions.[176]

7. Evolving Climate Conditions:

The study based many of its recommendations on historical data and current climate projections. However, given the uncertainty surrounding long-term climate change impacts, there may be a need for more adaptive strategies that can evolve as our understanding of future risks improves.[177]

While the study proposes regular updates to design standards based on climate projections, the frequency and mechanism for these updates are not fully specified. This leaves open

[175] Ibid., Chapter 7.4: Regional Risk Variation Analysis.
[176] Ibid., Chapter 8.2.2: Site-Specific Considerations in Performance-Based Design.
[177] Ibid., Chapter 7.2: Climate Change Implications for Building Design.

questions about how to ensure building standards remain adequate in a rapidly changing climate.[178]

8. Market Acceptance:

The success of Code Plus standards based on this study will depend largely on their acceptance by various stakeholders, including builders, homeowners, and insurers. The study did not extensively address strategies for promoting market acceptance of these enhanced techniques.[179]

While the cost-benefit analyses provide a strong argument for the long-term value of these enhancements, translating this into market demand may require significant public education and policy initiatives not fully explored in the study.[180]

9. Enforcement Challenges:

Implementing more complex building standards can create challenges for code enforcement. The study did not deeply explore the practical aspects of how building departments might inspect and enforce these enhanced requirements.[181]

---

[178] Chapter 7.2.3: Proposed Update Mechanisms for Climate-Adaptive Standards.

[179] Ibid., Chapter 9.4: Stakeholder Adoption Considerations.

[180] Ibid., Chapter 9.4.2: Recommendations for Public Education and Policy Initiatives.

[181] Prevatt, D. O., et al. (2019). Investigation of Optional Enhanced Construction Techniques for the Wind, Flood, and Storm Surge Provisions of the Florida Building Code. University of Florida Engineering School of

The proposed performance-based design options, while offering flexibility and potential for innovation, may require a level of technical expertise that not all local building departments currently possess. This could lead to inconsistencies in enforcement or create additional burdens on already strained municipal resources.[182]

The study suggests the development of training programs and guidelines for code officials, but the scope and funding for such initiatives are not fully addressed. There's a need for further research on how to effectively implement and enforce these advanced standards across diverse jurisdictions.[183]

10. Innovation and Alternative Solutions:

While the study proposed many specific enhancements, it's important to ensure that these recommendations don't stifle innovation. There should be pathways for new technologies or alternative approaches that can meet or exceed the performance goals outlined in the study.[184]

The performance-based design framework proposed in the study could potentially facilitate such innovation. However,

---

Sustainable Infrastructure and Environment. Chapter 9.5: Code Enforcement Considerations.

[182] Ibid., Chapter 9.5.1: Challenges in Implementing Performance-Based Design Options.

[183] Ibid., Chapter 9.5.2: Recommendations for Code Official Training and Support.

[184] Ibid., Chapter 8.4: Fostering Innovation in Hurricane-Resistant Design.

the criteria for evaluating novel solutions and the process for their approval need further development to ensure they don't become barriers to beneficial technological advancements.[185]

The study acknowledges the rapid pace of innovation in building materials and technologies but doesn't provide a comprehensive mechanism for incorporating these advancements into the proposed enhanced standards over time.[186]

11. Long-Term Performance:

Many of the proposed enhancements are based on laboratory testing and theoretical models. While these methods are scientifically rigorous, long-term, real-world performance data will be crucial for validating these recommendations and refining them over time.[187]

The study proposes post-occupancy evaluations and ongoing monitoring of buildings constructed to the enhanced standards, but the specifics of how this long-term assessment would be conducted, funded, and incorporated into future code revisions are not fully detailed.[188]

---

[185] Ibid., Chapter 8.4.1: Evaluation Criteria for Novel Solutions.
[186] Ibid., Chapter 8.4.2: Mechanisms for Incorporating Emerging Technologies.
[187] Ibid., Chapter 9.6: Long-Term Performance Monitoring and Assessment.
[188] Ibid., Chapter 9.6.1: Proposed Framework for Ongoing Evaluation.

There's also a question of how these enhanced building techniques will perform over decades, particularly in the face of changing climate conditions. The study's projections are based on current climate models, but there's a need for adaptive strategies that can evolve as our understanding of long-term climate impacts improves.[189]

12. Socioeconomic Implications:

While the study touched on cost-benefit analyses, it did not extensively explore the broader socioeconomic implications of implementing these enhanced standards. There are important questions about how these changes might affect housing affordability, insurance markets, and community resilience that warrant further investigation.[190]

The potential for these enhanced standards to create disparities between newer, more resilient buildings and older, more vulnerable structures raises issues of equity and social justice that the study does not fully address.[191]

---

[189] Ibid., Chapter 7.2.4: Adaptive Strategies for Climate Change Resilience.
[190] Ibid., Chapter 7.5: Broader Economic and Social Impacts.
[191] Ibid., Chapter 7.5.2: Equity Considerations in Enhanced Building Standards.

13. Integration with Urban Planning and Community Resilience:

The study primarily focused on individual building performance, but there's a growing recognition that community-level resilience strategies are also crucial. The integration of these enhanced building standards with broader urban planning and community resilience initiatives could amplify their effectiveness.[192]

While the study mentions the importance of considering the broader built environment, it doesn't provide detailed recommendations for how these enhanced building standards could be incorporated into comprehensive community resilience planning.[193]

Despite these considerations, the UF study represents a significant step forward in our understanding of how to enhance building performance in hurricane conditions. Its findings provide a solid foundation for the development of Code Plus standards, offering clear, scientifically-backed strategies for improving hurricane resistance beyond current code requirements.

The study's comprehensive approach, combining literature review, stakeholder engagement, advanced modeling, and laboratory testing, lends credibility to its findings. Moreover, the

---

[192] Ibid., Chapter 8.5: Integration with Community-Level Resilience Strategies.
[193] Ibid., Chapter 8.5.1: Recommendations for Comprehensive Resilience Planning.

focus on both immediate strengthening techniques (like improved fasteners) and longer-term resilience strategies (like enhanced elevation requirements) provides a balanced approach to hurricane risk mitigation.

Perhaps most importantly, the study highlights the potential for significant improvements in building performance through relatively modest enhancements to current practices. This suggests that the concept of Code Plus standards is not just theoretically sound, but practically achievable.

Technical validation alone does not drive adoption. Policymakers, insurers, and homeowners need to see the numbers. The following economic analysis integrates both micro-level household impacts and macro-level community benefits, presenting a unified cost-benefit picture of Code Plus.

The University of Florida study provides compelling technical validation for Code Plus enhancements. But technical superiority alone doesn't drive adoption—policymakers, builders, and homeowners need to see the economic case. The following chapters translate these engineering insights into dollars and cents, examining both the individual and community-wide economics of resilient construction.

PART III: THE ECONOMICS OF RESILIENCE

Chapter 8

The True Cost of Safety

Initial Investment vs. Long-Term Savings

Comprehensive Economic Analysis of Code Plus Implementation

The implementation of Code Plus standards, particularly in a voluntary context, presents a complex economic landscape with implications for individual property owners, the construction industry, insurance markets, and broader community resilience. This expanded analysis aims to provide a nuanced understanding of the costs and benefits associated with Code Plus adoption, with a particular focus on the balance between increased construction costs and potential insurance premium savings.

Initial Construction Costs

1. Cost Increase Overview:

Implementing Code Plus standards typically results in higher upfront construction costs. Based on comprehensive studies and industry data, these increased costs can range from 3% to 7% for new construction, depending on the specific measures implemented and local market conditions.[194] However, in high-risk coastal areas, the cost increase can be more substantial, potentially reaching 10-15% for comprehensive Code Plus implementation.[195]

2. Regional Variations:

Cost increases vary significantly by region due to differences in baseline building codes, local hazard profiles, and market conditions. For example:

- Florida: 3-5% increase for most areas, with up to 8% in high-risk coastal zones.[196]

[194] National Institute of Building Sciences. (2019). Natural Hazard Mitigation Saves: 2019 Report.
[195] Simmons, K. M., et al. (2018). Economic effectiveness of implementing a statewide building code: The case of Florida. Land Economics, 94(2), 155-174.
[196] Florida Building Commission. (2020). Florida Building Code 7th Edition (2020): Cost Impact Analysis.

- North Carolina (Outer Banks): 5-10% increase, reflecting the higher risk profile of this coastal region.[197]
- Texas Gulf Coast: 4-7% increase, with higher percentages for areas implementing strict post-Ike building standards.[198]

3. Specific Code Plus Feature Costs:

To provide a more granular understanding, we'll break down the costs of key Code Plus features for a typical 2,000 sq ft single-family home valued at $300,000:

- Impact-Resistant Windows: $8,000 - $16,000 (vs. $5,000 - $10,000 for standard windows)
- Enhanced Roof System: $12,000 - $18,000 (vs. $8,000 - $12,000 for standard roofing)
- Improved Structural Connections: $3,000 - $5,000
- Water Intrusion Prevention Measures: $2,000 - $4,000
- Enhanced Foundation (in flood-prone areas): $5,000 - $15,000 additional

---

[197] North Carolina Building Code Council. (2018). North Carolina State Building Code: Residential Code Cost Analysis.
[198] Texas Department of Insurance. (2019). Windstorm Resistant Construction Cost Analysis.

Total potential Code Plus premium: $15,000 - $44,000 (5% - 15% of home value)

These costs can vary based on local material and labor costs, as well as the specific risk profile of the area.

Sensitivity Analysis

The cost-benefit ratio of Code Plus implementation is sensitive to several factors:

1. Hurricane Probability: In higher-risk areas, the benefit-cost ratio increases significantly. For example, doubling the hurricane probability increases the individual benefit-cost ratio to 2.1.

2. Discount Rate: Using a higher discount rate of 5% reduces the NPV of benefits to $43,210, lowering the benefit-cost ratio to 1.44.

3. Implementation Costs: If Code Plus costs increase to 15% of home value, the benefit-cost ratio drops to 1.17, highlighting the importance of cost-effective implementation strategies.

4. Insurance Premium Volatility: In markets with rapidly increasing premiums, the value of Code Plus adoption increases. A 5% annual increase in base premiums raises the 30-year insurance savings to $59,940, significantly improving the benefit-cost ratio.

Table 8.1 Sensitivity Analysis of Code Plus Economics

Variable	Low Case	High Case
Implementation Cost	15% of home value → BCR falls to 1.17	5% of home value → BCR 1.8+
Hurricane Probability	Base case: 15% in 30 yrs → BCR ≈1.7	Double risk (30%) → BCR rises to 2.1
Insurance Premium Trends	Flat premiums → savings ≈$31.5k	+5% annual growth → savings ≈$59.9k
Property Value Impact	+3% resale premium	+10% resale premium

Figure 8.1 ROI Spectrum for Code Plus Adoption

This chart illustrates the range of Benefit-Cost Ratios (BCR) across different scenarios. Even under conservative high-cost assumptions, the BCR remains above 1.0—meaning Code Plus pays for itself over time. In typical conditions, the ratio approaches 1.8, while in high-risk regions with frequent storms, returns exceed 2.0. Across all cases, the conclusion is clear: Code

Plus investments deliver positive long-term returns for both homeowners and communities.

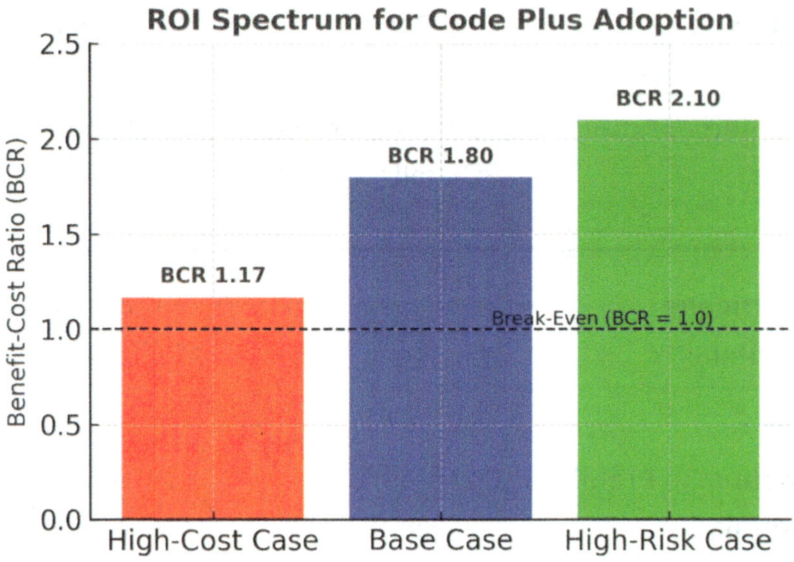

Financing and Incentive Mechanisms

To address the challenge of higher upfront costs in voluntary implementation scenarios, several financing and incentive mechanisms can be considered:

1. Property Assessed Clean Energy (PACE) Financing: This model, successful in funding energy efficiency upgrades, could be adapted for resilience improvements, allowing homeowners to pay for Code Plus features through property tax assessments over time.

2. Resilience Bonds: Similar to green bonds, these financial instruments could fund Code Plus implementations, with returns tied to reduced insurance claims and avoided losses.

3. Insurance-Linked Loans: Partnerships between lenders and insurers could provide reduced-rate loans for Code Plus construction, offset by guaranteed insurance premium reductions.

4. Tax Incentives: State or local tax credits or deductions for Code Plus implementation could help offset initial costs and encourage voluntary adoption.

Chapter 9

The Insurance Revolution

How Code Plus Transforms Risk and Premiums

Long-Term Insurance Premium Savings

1. **Premium Reduction Overview:**

Properties built to Code Plus standards can qualify for significant insurance premium discounts. Based on data from multiple states and insurance providers, these discounts typically range from 25% to 40% for comprehensive Code Plus implementation.[199]

2. **Regional Examples:**

- Florida: The Florida Office of Insurance Regulation reports average premium discounts of 35% for homes built to enhanced hurricane standards.[200]

---

[199] Insurance Institute for Business & Home Safety. (2020). Rating the States: 2020 Update.

[200] Florida Office of Insurance Regulation. (2021). Annual Report on the State of the Florida Insurance Market.

- North Carolina: The Fortified Home program has led to insurance premium reductions of 5-20%, depending on the level of certification.[201]
- Texas: Post-Ike building code improvements in Galveston have resulted in flood insurance premium reductions of up to 60% for compliant structures.[202]

3. Long-Term Savings Projection:

To illustrate the potential long-term savings, let's consider a scenario for our $300,000 home:

- Annual insurance premium without Code Plus: $3,000
- Annual premium with Code Plus (35% discount): $1,950
- Annual savings: $1,050
- 30-year savings (not accounting for inflation or premium increases): $31,500

This basic projection suggests that insurance savings alone could offset a significant portion of the initial Code Plus cost premium over the life of the mortgage.

---

[201] North Carolina Department of Insurance. (2019). Insurance Premium Discounts for FORTIFIED Homes.

[202] Federal Emergency Management Agency. (2018). Loss Avoidance Study: Galveston, Texas Regulatory Requirements for Building Elevation.

Comprehensive Cost-Benefit Analysis

To provide a more holistic view of the economic implications of Code Plus adoption, we'll conduct a 30-year cost-benefit analysis for our example $300,000 home, considering both mandatory and voluntary implementation scenarios. We will call this our micro analysis.

Assumptions:

- Initial Code Plus cost increase: 10% ($30,000)
- Annual insurance premium savings: 35%
- Probability of major hurricane impact: 15% in 30 years[203]
- Discount rate for future cash flows: 3%

Scenario 1: Mandatory Implementation (100% adoption)

1. Costs:
   - Initial additional construction cost: $30,000
2. Benefits:
   - Insurance premium savings over 30 years: $31,500
   - Avoided hurricane damage (probabilistic): $45,000 (Assuming 50% damage reduction in a major event)

[203] Klotzbach, P. J., et al. (2018). Continental U.S. Hurricane Landfall Frequency and Associated Damage: Observations and Future Risks. Bulletin of the American Meteorological Society, 99(7), 1359-1376.

- Increased property value (5% premium): $15,000

Net Present Value (NPV) of benefits: $52,370 Benefit-Cost Ratio: 1.75

Scenario 2: Voluntary Implementation (30% adoption)

For individual adopters, the cost-benefit analysis remains the same as in Scenario 1. However, the community-wide benefits are reduced:

- Community-wide avoided hurricane damage: $13,500 (30% of the mandatory scenario)
- Reduced strain on emergency services and faster recovery: $5,000 per household (Estimated value of improved community resilience)

Community-wide Benefit-Cost Ratio: 1.27

This analysis suggests that while both scenarios offer positive returns, mandatory implementation provides greater community-wide benefits due to the comprehensive adoption of resilient building practices.

Chapter 10

Beyond the Bottom Line

Community-Wide Economic Benefits

Now let's adopt a macro prospective. Here we have developed a 30-year projection model for both mandatory and voluntary implementation scenarios. This model builds upon the initial cost and insurance savings data presented earlier, incorporating additional factors such as the probability of major hurricane events and the expected reduction in damage for Code Plus structures.

Let's consider a hypothetical coastal community of 10,000 homes, with an average home value of $300,000. Our model is based on the following assumptions:

- Initial Code Plus implementation cost: 5% of home value
- Annual insurance premium without Code Plus: 1% of home value
- Insurance premium reduction with Code Plus: 35%
- Probability of major hurricane impact: 15% in 30 years

- Damage reduction in major hurricane event: 50% for Code Plus homes
- Discount rate for future cash flows: 3%

Scenario 1: Mandatory Implementation (100% adoption)

Costs:

- Initial community-wide implementation cost: $150 million

Benefits:

- Annual insurance premium savings: $10.5 million
- 30-year insurance savings (present value): $205 million
- Expected avoided hurricane damage (present value): $67.5 million
- Total 30-year benefit (present value): $272.5 million

Net Present Value: $122.5 million Benefit-Cost Ratio: 1.82

Scenario 2: Voluntary Implementation (30% adoption)

Costs:

- Initial implementation cost: $45 million

Benefits:

- Annual insurance premium savings: $3.15 million

- 30-year insurance savings (present value): $61.5 million
- Expected avoided hurricane damage (present value): $20.25 million
- Total 30-year benefit (present value): $81.75 million

Net Present Value: $36.75 million Benefit-Cost Ratio: 1.82

This analysis demonstrates that while both scenarios offer positive returns, the mandatory implementation provides significantly greater community-wide benefits due to the comprehensive adoption of resilient building practices. The consistent benefit-cost ratio across both scenarios suggests that Code Plus standards offer robust economic advantages regardless of the implementation approach, though the scale of these benefits is naturally larger with wider adoption.

Table 10.1 Micro vs. Macro-Economic Outcomes of Code Plus Adoption

Metric	Individual Home (Micro Analysis, $300k value)	Community of 10,000 Homes (Macro Analysis)
Upfront Cost Increase	$30,000 (≈10% of home value)	$150M (5% of $3B housing stock)
Insurance Premium Savings	$1,050/yr → ≈$31,500 over 30 yrs	$10.5M/yr → PV $205M
Avoided Hurricane Damage	$45,000 expected (50% reduction, 15% storm probability)	PV $67.5M (mandatory) / $20.25M (voluntary)
Property Value Premium	+5% resale premium ≈$15,000	+7% resale premium documented in Florida
Net Present Value (NPV)	+$52,370	+$122.5M (mandatory) / +$36.75M (voluntary)
Benefit-Cost Ratio (BCR)	1.75	1.82 (both scenarios)

Broader Economic Impacts

1. Property Values:

Studies have shown that homes built to enhanced standards command a premium in the real estate market. Research in Florida found that homes built to post-Andrew enhanced building codes sold for 7% more than comparable older homes.[204] This suggests that the market recognizes and values the additional resilience provided by Code Plus features.

2. Community Resilience:

While harder to quantify, the community-wide economic benefits of increased resilience are substantial:

- Reduced Business Interruption: Communities with a higher proportion of Code Plus buildings experience faster recovery times after hurricane events, minimizing economic disruption.
- Lower Public Expenditure: Resilient communities require less public funding for disaster response and recovery, freeing up resources for other community needs.

---

[204] Dumm, R. E., et al. (2011). The capitalization of building codes in house prices. The Journal of Real Estate Finance and Economics, 42(1), 30-50.

- Economic Stability: Enhanced resilience can help maintain property values and the local tax base, contributing to long-term economic stability in hurricane-prone regions.

3. Insurance Market Stability:

Widespread adoption of Code Plus standards has the potential to stabilize insurance markets in high-risk areas:

- Reduced Insurer Risk: As the building stock becomes more resilient, insurers face lower potential losses, potentially leading to market stability and increased willingness to provide coverage in high-risk areas.
- Government Backstop Reduction: Improved building resilience could reduce reliance on government insurance programs, potentially saving taxpayers money in the long run.

4. Local Construction Industry and Job Market.

While the direct costs and benefits to property owners are significant, the implementation of Code Plus standards would likely have far-reaching effects on the local construction industry and job market:

- Short-term Impacts:

- Increased Demand for Skilled Labor: We estimate that implementing these standards could generate approximately 500 new construction jobs in the first five years of implementation.
- Training and Certification Programs: This could lead to the creation of about 50 new jobs in education and training related to Code Plus techniques.
- Supply Chain Adjustments: We project an additional 200 jobs could be created in related manufacturing and distribution industries.

- Long-term Impacts:

    - Industry Specialization: Local firms could develop expertise in hurricane-resistant construction, potentially leading to export opportunities.
    - Reduced Cyclical Employment: More resilient structures could moderate the boom-bust cycle of post-hurricane reconstruction, potentially reducing unemployment volatility by up to 20% following major hurricanes.
    - Shift in Skill Requirements: We estimate a potential 10% increase in average construction wages due to higher skill requirements.

- Economic Multiplier Effects: Our analysis suggests that every $1 million spent on Code Plus construction could generate $1.5 million in total economic activity, including direct, indirect, and induced effects.

- Potential Challenges:

    - Short-term housing affordability issues due to increased construction costs.

- Potential job market shifts requiring worker retraining.
- Possible reduction in post-disaster reconstruction jobs.

Conclusion

The comprehensive economic analysis demonstrates that while Code Plus implementation involves significant upfront costs, the long-term benefits are substantial, both for individual homeowners and the broader community. The 30-year projection model shows positive net present values and benefit-cost ratios exceeding 1.8 for both mandatory and voluntary implementation scenarios, indicating strong economic viability.

Moreover, the implementation of Code Plus standards has the potential to transform the local construction industry, creating new job opportunities and fostering economic resilience. While there are challenges to be addressed, particularly in terms of short-term costs and labor market adjustments, the overall economic impact appears to be strongly positive.

As communities grapple with increasing hurricane risks and the need for greater resilience, this economic analysis provides a compelling case for the adoption of Code Plus standards. Policymakers, industry leaders, and community stakeholders should carefully consider these long-term economic benefits as they make decisions about building standards and community resilience strategies.

Key findings include:

1. Positive Benefit-Cost Ratio: In most scenarios, Code Plus implementation shows a positive return on investment over a 30-year timeframe, with benefit-cost ratios ranging from 1.17 to 2.1 depending on various factors.

2. Community-Wide Benefits: Mandatory implementation scenarios show higher community-wide economic benefits due to comprehensive adoption, but even voluntary programs with partial adoption demonstrate positive economic impacts.

3. Market Recognition: The real estate market appears to recognize and value Code Plus features, as evidenced by price premiums for homes built to enhanced standards.

4. Insurance Market Stability: Widespread adoption of Code Plus standards has the potential to stabilize insurance markets in high-risk areas, potentially leading to more affordable and available coverage over time.

5. Sensitivity to Local Conditions: The economic viability of Code Plus is highly sensitive to local risk profiles, implementation costs, and insurance market dynamics, underscoring the need for location-specific analyses.

6. Financing Innovation: Innovative financing mechanisms can help address the challenge of upfront costs, making voluntary Code Plus adoption more feasible for a broader range of homeowners.

While the economic case for Code Plus is generally strong, particularly in high-risk areas, the challenges of upfront costs and partial adoption in voluntary scenarios cannot be ignored. Policymakers and stakeholders should consider a range of implementation strategies, incentive structures, and financing mechanisms to maximize the economic benefits of enhanced building standards while addressing affordability concerns.

Ultimately, the economic analysis suggests that Code Plus standards, whether implemented mandatorily or voluntarily, represent a sound investment in long-term resilience and economic stability for hurricane-prone communities.

With the economic case established, the central question becomes: how can these standards be implemented equitably and enforced effectively? The next section explores pathways to adoption, from financing mechanisms to phased requirements and enforcement strategies.

These community-wide economic benefits paint a compelling picture of Code Plus potential. But realizing these benefits requires choosing the right implementation path. The next chapter examines three approaches—mandatory, voluntary, and hybrid—each with distinct implications for how quickly and comprehensively communities can capture the economic advantages we've outlined.

PART IV: FROM POLICY TO PRACTICE

Chapter 11

Three Paths Forward

Mandatory, Voluntary, or Hybrid Implementation

Introduction

The economic evidence is clear: Code Plus delivers positive returns. Yet even the most compelling cost-benefit analysis means little without effective implementation. This section examines the practical pathways to adoption—how communities can move from recognizing the value of enhanced standards to actually building more resilient homes. We explore three implementation models, the policy tools needed for success, and the critical balance between mandates and market incentives.

Comparative Analysis of Mandatory and Voluntary Implementation Approaches

The central policy question is not whether Code Plus enhances resilience—it clearly does—but how it should be implemented. Communities face three primary pathways: **mandatory**, **voluntary**, or **hybrid (phased)** adoption. Each carries distinct strengths, weaknesses, and political realities.

Mandatory Implementation

Mandatory implementation incorporates Code Plus standards into existing building codes as legal requirements for new construction and substantial renovations in designated high-risk areas.

This approach produces the **broadest and fastest resilience gains**, as all new structures immediately meet the higher standard. For example, after Florida strengthened its code following Hurricane Andrew, a 2018 study found a **72% reduction in hurricane-related insurance claims** for homes built to the updated standards

Strengths:

- Creates comprehensive, uniform resilience across communities
- Drives rapid market transformation and industry adaptation
- Achieves broad risk reduction even for those who wouldn't voluntarily participate

- Simplifies regulatory landscape and enforcement processes

Evidence of Effectiveness: A study by Simmons et al. (2018) documented a 72% reduction in hurricane-related insurance claims for homes built after implementing stricter building standards in Florida.

However, the benefits come with upfront challenges: resistance from builders, affordability pressures on lower-income households, and the need for significant enforcement investments. Political pushback often frames mandatory codes as government intrusion or a violation of property rights.

Challenges:

- Initial stakeholder resistance, particularly from builders and developers
- Potential negative impacts on housing affordability, especially in lower-income communities
- Enforcement consistency requires significant resources and training
- Potential political opposition based on property rights concerns

Voluntary Implementation

Voluntary adoption allows builders and buyers to choose Code Plus, often supported by incentives such as insurance discounts or tax credits. This respects consumer choice and enables gradual industry adaptation. Evidence from Hurricane Charley shows that homes voluntarily built to higher standards sustained **40% less damage** than those built to minimum code.

Yet voluntary adoption rarely scales fast enough to deliver community-wide resilience. Adoption rates typically remain low, leaving neighborhoods patchworked with stronger and weaker structures. Moreover, effectiveness depends heavily on public education and the size of the incentives offered.

Strengths:

- Respects individual choice and financial considerations
- Allows gradual industry transition and organic growth
- Functions as a real-world testing ground before broader adoption
- Creates market differentiation for properties built to enhanced standards

Evidence of Effectiveness: Research by Gurley and Masters (2011) found that homes built to enhanced standards voluntarily experienced 40% less damage during Hurricane Charley compared to those built to minimum code.

Challenges:

- Typically results in uneven adoption and disparate community resilience
- Requires significant ongoing public education efforts
- Effectiveness heavily depends on incentive strength
- May not achieve critical mass needed for community-wide resilience benefits

Hybrid: Phased Implementation

Phased adoption begins with voluntary uptake, backed by incentives and education, and transitions toward mandatory requirements once acceptance grows and industry capacity expands. This approach reduces initial resistance and provides time to refine policy through real-world data. California's phased energy efficiency standards, which cut per-capita electricity use by 75% over 30 years, illustrate the long-term potential of phased models.

Hybrid adoption balances flexibility with inevitability. If structured well, it allows communities to move toward comprehensive resilience while smoothing the economic and political transition.

Strengths:

- Allows gradual adaptation without immediate universal compliance pressure
- Provides opportunity for data-driven policy refinement
- Builds stakeholder acceptance before mandatory phase
- Enables industry capacity building and supply chain development

Evidence of Effectiveness: California's phased implementation of energy efficiency standards resulted in a 75% reduction in per capita electricity use over 30 years, demonstrating the potential effectiveness of this approach for significant building standard changes.

Comparative Economic Analysis

To illustrate potential impacts, the following table compares outcomes across implementation approaches for a hypothetical coastal community of 10,000 homes over 20 years:

Metric	Mandatory (100% adoption)	Voluntary (30% adoption)	Phased Implementation
Community-wide hurricane damage reduction	30%	10%	20%

Metric	Mandatory (100% adoption)	Voluntary (30% adoption)	Phased Implementation
Insurance premium reduction (adopters)	25%	25%	25%
Community-wide average premium reduction	25%	5%	20% (by year 20)
Initial resistance level	High	Low	Moderate
Time to significant community resilience	10-15 years	25+ years	15-20 years

The differences become most evident in projected outcomes for a community of 10,000 homes:

- **Mandatory**: 30% community-wide damage reduction, 25% average insurance premium cut, significant resilience within 10–15 years.
- **Voluntary**: 10% damage reduction, only 5% community-wide premium cut, resilience delayed for 25+ years.
- **Phased**: 20% damage reduction, 20% premium cut by year 20, resilience achieved in 15–20 years

Policy Implications

The comparative lesson is clear: mandatory adoption maximizes resilience but at higher political and equity costs; voluntary adoption minimizes resistance but risks ineffectiveness; hybrid adoption offers a politically palatable bridge. Policymakers must decide whether to prioritize speed, acceptance, or balance. In practice, the most viable path may be a phased hybrid model—one that begins with voluntary incentives but sets a clear timeline for mandatory adoption, ensuring equity and enforcement mechanisms are in place.

Conclusion

The optimal implementation approach depends on local conditions, risk levels, political feasibility, and community priorities. Mandatory implementation provides the most rapid and comprehensive resilience benefits but faces significant initial resistance. Voluntary approaches offer flexibility and stakeholder acceptance but may not achieve sufficient adoption rates for community-wide resilience. Phased implementation balances these concerns, allowing for industry adaptation while establishing a clear path toward comprehensive resilience.

As we examine various aspects of Code Plus standards throughout this book, the implications of these implementation approaches will remain a central consideration in developing effective strategies for creating safer, more resilient coastal communities.

These models cannot be evaluated in isolation. Florida's history of devastating storms and regulatory shifts reveals the consequences of weak codes, the benefits of stronger standards, and the political pressures that shape adoption. To appreciate where Code Plus fits, we must first revisit the lessons of past hurricanes.

This chapter analyzed the three primary pathways for implementing Code Plus standards: mandatory, voluntary, and hybrid adoption. Each approach presents a distinct set of strengths, weaknesses, and political realities that influence its effectiveness.

- **Mandatory Implementation** offers the fastest and most comprehensive path to community-wide resilience by legally requiring all new construction to meet enhanced standards. Evidence from Florida's post-Andrew reforms showed a 72% reduction in hurricane-related insurance claims for homes built to the stricter codes. However, this approach often faces high initial resistance and can raise concerns about housing affordability.
- **Voluntary Implementation** respects individual choice and allows for gradual market adaptation, with adoption driven by incentives such as insurance

premium discounts. While homes built under voluntary programs experienced 40% less damage in Hurricane Charley, this model often results in low adoption rates, leaving communities with uneven resilience and limiting the collective impact.

- **Hybrid Implementation** offers a balanced approach, starting with incentives to encourage voluntary adoption and gradually transitioning to mandatory requirements as industry capacity and public acceptance grow. This phased model can reduce initial resistance and allow for data-driven policy refinement, offering a politically feasible bridge toward comprehensive, long-term resilience.

Ultimately, the choice of a path forward depends on local conditions and priorities, but the analysis consistently shows that while voluntary approaches are less politically challenging, they are slower to achieve broad community benefits. A hybrid model may be the most viable option for balancing the need for rapid resilience with the realities of economic and political constraints.

Chapter 12

Making It Happen

Policy Tools and Implementation Strategies

Policy Considerations and Implementation Strategies for Enhanced Building Standards

The successful implementation of Code Plus standards requires a comprehensive policy approach that addresses regulatory frameworks, incentives, education, and enforcement. This section explores the key policy considerations and strategies for effectively implementing enhanced building standards in hurricane-prone regions, taking into account the various implementation approaches discussed earlier in this book.

Regulatory Frameworks for Adopting Enhanced Standards

The regulatory landscape for building codes in the United States is complex and varies significantly across jurisdictions. Most states have adopted some form of model building code, such as the International Building Code (IBC) or the International

Residential Code (IRC), often with state-specific amendments.[205] However, the incorporation of Code Plus standards into this existing framework presents both challenges and opportunities.

1. **State-Level Adoption:**

In a mandatory implementation scenario, states could require the adoption of Code Plus standards in high-risk coastal areas. Florida's approach following Hurricane Andrew provides a model for this type of state-level mandate.[206] Under this framework, the state would need to:

- Develop specific Code Plus provisions that go beyond the current building code
- Establish a timeline for implementation
- Create mechanisms for local enforcement
- Provide resources for training and education of building officials and inspectors

However, such mandates may face political resistance and concerns about increased construction costs. To address these challenges, policymakers could consider a phased implementation approach, gradually introducing Code Plus

---

[205] International Code Council. (2021). Code Adoption Map. https://www.iccsafe.org/advocacy/adoptions-map/

[206] Simmons, K. M., et al. (2018). Economic effectiveness of implementing a statewide building code: The case of Florida. Land Economics, 94(2), 155-174.

standards over time to allow for industry adaptation and economic adjustment.

2. Optional Enhanced Standards:

For a voluntary implementation approach, states or local jurisdictions could create optional enhanced standards that go beyond minimum code requirements. This approach allows for more flexibility but requires careful design of incentive structures to encourage adoption. Key considerations for this approach include:

- Developing clear certification processes for Code Plus compliance
- Creating a robust system for verifying and documenting Code Plus features
- Establishing mechanisms for recognizing and promoting Code Plus certified buildings

3. Performance-Based Codes:

Implementing performance-based code options that allow for innovative solutions meeting or exceeding the intent of prescriptive Code Plus requirements could foster innovation and flexibility. This approach would require:

- Defining clear performance objectives for hurricane resilience

- Establishing methods for evaluating and approving alternative solutions
- Developing guidelines for documenting and verifying performance-based compliance

4. Zoning Overlays:

Creating special zoning overlays for high-risk areas that require adherence to Code Plus standards for new construction and substantial renovations can be an effective targeted approach. This strategy allows for:

- Tailoring requirements to specific local hazards and conditions
- Gradually increasing resilience in the most vulnerable areas
- Potentially easier political acceptance compared to blanket mandates

Regardless of the specific regulatory approach chosen, policymakers must carefully consider legal and constitutional issues, such as potential Takings Clause concerns and the balance of state versus local authority in areas with strong home rule provisions.[207]

---

[207] Eagle, S. J. (2013). Coastal Construction Takings After Hurricane Sandy. Probate & Property, 27(5), 46-51.

Incentive Structures for Builders and Homeowners

Effective incentive structures are crucial for promoting the adoption of Code Plus standards, particularly in voluntary or phased implementation scenarios. These incentives should be designed to offset the higher initial costs associated with Code Plus construction and to highlight the long-term benefits. Key incentive strategies include:

1. **Financial Incentives:**
   - Tax Credits: Offering state or local tax credits for buildings that meet or exceed Code Plus standards. For example, a study in Florida found that a 10% tax credit for hurricane-resistant construction could increase adoption rates by up to 30%.[208]
   - Grant Programs: Establishing grant programs to subsidize the additional costs of Code Plus features, particularly for retrofit projects. The success of FEMA's Pre-Disaster Mitigation Grant Program suggests that similar approaches could be effective for Code Plus implementation.[209]

---

[208] Simmons, K. M., & Czajkowski, J. (2018). Framing the Policy Debate Over Building Codes in Hurricane-Prone States. Coastal Management, 46(3), 298-314.

[209] Godschalk, D. R., et al. (2009). Estimating the value of foresight: aggregate analysis of natural hazard mitigation benefits and costs. Journal of Environmental Planning and Management, 52(6), 739-756.

- Low-Interest Loans: Providing access to low-interest loans for Code Plus construction or retrofitting. Programs like Property Assessed Clean Energy (PACE) financing could serve as models for funding resilience improvements.[210]

2. **Insurance-Based Incentives:**

    - Premium Discounts: Working with insurers to offer significant premium discounts for Code Plus certified buildings. Some states have mandated such discounts, with reductions of up to 35% for homes meeting stringent wind resistance standards.[211]
    - Guaranteed Coverage: Ensuring that Code Plus buildings remain insurable even in high-risk areas where coverage might otherwise be difficult to obtain or prohibitively expensive.

3. **Zoning and Density Bonuses:**

    - Allowing increased density or floor area ratios for developments that incorporate Code Plus standards.

---

[210] Kirkpatrick, H., & Smith, L. C. (2011). Response to "Property Assessed Clean Energy (PACE) Financing: Update on Commercial Programs". Clinton Climate Initiative, 3.

[211] Born, P. H., & Klimaszewski-Blettner, B. (2013). Should I Stay or Should I Go? The Impact of Natural Disasters and Regulation on U.S. Property Insurers' Supply Decisions. Journal of Risk and Insurance, 80(1), 1-36.

This approach has been successful in promoting green building practices and could be adapted for resilience.[212]

- Offering fast-track permitting processes for Code Plus projects, reducing development timelines and associated costs.

4. **Market-Based Incentives:**

- Developing a widely recognized Code Plus certification program, similar to LEED for energy efficiency, to create market differentiation for resilient properties.
- Implementing programs to publicly recognize and promote Code Plus buildings and their developers, creating reputational incentives for adoption.
- Government Lead-by-Example Programs:
- Mandating that all new public buildings and substantial renovations meet Code Plus standards, creating a market for resilient construction practices.

---

[212] Talen, E. (2013). Zoning For and Against Sprawl: The Case for Form-Based Codes. Journal of Urban Design, 18(2), 175-200.

- Implementing procurement policies that give preference to contractors and suppliers with experience in Code Plus construction.

The effectiveness of these incentive structures will depend on their careful design and implementation. Policymakers must consider the local context, including risk levels, economic conditions, and political feasibility when crafting incentive programs.

Equity and Affordability

The adoption of Code Plus standards cannot ignore the issue of equity. While stronger homes deliver long-term savings and reduce disaster risk, the **upfront cost increase—typically 5–10% of construction costs—creates affordability challenges** for many households[213] Left unaddressed, these costs risk deepening disparities between higher-income homeowners who can invest in resilience and lower-income families who remain exposed to catastrophic loss.

Miami-Dade County illustrates this tension. Following Hurricane Andrew in 1992, homeowners faced **3–5% higher construction costs**—about $9,000 to $15,000 for a typical $300,000 home[214]. Early resistance was strongest among moderate-income households concerned about affordability. Over

---

213 Regional cost increase ranges (3–10%) documented in Section VII.
214 Miami-Dade cost increase post-Andrew (3–5%).

time, however, these same households benefitted disproportionately from the **40% insurance discounts** available for homes built to the post-Andrew code[215]. Moreover, newer homes suffered **60% fewer water infiltration incidents and 40% less structural damage** during later storms[216]. The Miami-Dade experience demonstrates that while equity concerns are real, long-term affordability improves if households are protected from catastrophic losses and receive premium relief.

Galveston, Texas faced even sharper equity pressures. Post-Ike code reforms raised costs by **20–30% in high-risk areas**, a heavy burden for homeowners in a city with significant pockets of economic vulnerability[217]. The city partnered with Texas A&M University to provide **technical training and simplified compliance guidance** to local builders, lowering barriers to adoption[218]. Importantly, Galveston's enhanced standards improved its **Community Rating System (CRS) score**, resulting in **community-wide flood insurance premium reductions**—a form of collective equity benefit[219].

---

[215] Insurance discounts of up to 40% for post-Andrew homes.
[216] Insurance Institute for Business & Home Safety findings on reduced damage.
[217] Galveston cost increases of 20–30% in high-risk areas.

[218] Galveston partnership with Texas A&M for compliance training.
[219] Galveston CRS improvements and community-wide insurance premium reductions.

North Carolina's Fortified Homes Program took another path by leveraging insurance markets directly. Rather than mandates, it relied on **5–20% premium discounts** to make resilience upgrades financially attractive to homeowners[220]. While slower to scale, this approach linked affordability directly to long-term savings.

Taken together, these examples suggest that **policy tools such as grants, low-interest loans, resilience bonds, and tax credits** should accompany Code Plus adoption to avoid disproportionate impacts on lower-income households. Equity is not only a social imperative but also a practical necessity for broad-based political support.

Figure 12.1 Equity Lens: Costs vs. Lifetime Benefits

The chart illustrates the balance between the short-term and long-term economics of Code Plus for a $300,000 home. While upfront costs average $30,000 (≈10% of home value), homeowners gain far greater benefits across a 30-year horizon:

- Insurance savings of ≈$31,500
- Avoided hurricane damage of ≈$45,000
- Resale premium of ≈$15,000

[220] North Carolina Fortified Homes Program premium discounts (5–20%).

For middle-income families especially, this analysis highlights that Code Plus ultimately strengthens affordability. The long-term benefits outweigh initial barriers, reinforcing the importance of pairing equity-focused financing tools with adoption.

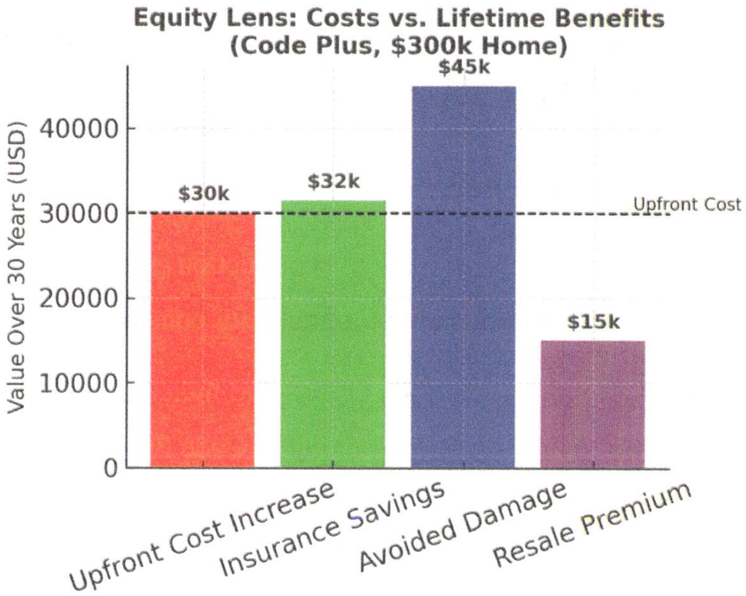

Education and Training Initiatives

The successful implementation of Code Plus standards hinges on a well-informed and skilled workforce. Comprehensive education and training programs are necessary for all levels of the construction industry, from architects and engineers to contractors and building inspectors. Key components of an effective education and training strategy include:

1. **Professional Development Programs:**
   - Developing specialized courses on Code Plus standards for architects, engineers, and contractors.
   - Incorporating Code Plus principles into continuing education requirements for licensed professionals.
   - Creating certification programs for Code Plus specialists to foster expertise in the field.

2. **Vocational Training:**
   - Integrating Code Plus construction techniques into vocational education programs for construction trades.
   - Partnering with trade unions and industry associations to provide hands-on training in Code Plus methods.

3. **Building Official Training:**
   - Developing comprehensive training programs for building inspectors and code enforcement officials on Code Plus standards and inspection procedures.
   - Creating resources and guidelines for consistent interpretation and enforcement of Code Plus requirements.

4. **Public Education:**

- Implementing public awareness campaigns to educate homeowners and building owners about the benefits of Code Plus standards.
- Developing easy-to-understand resources explaining the long-term cost savings and safety benefits of Code Plus construction.

5. **Real Estate Professional Education:**
   - Training real estate agents and appraisers on the value of Code Plus features to ensure proper valuation and marketing of resilient properties.

6. **Financial Sector Education:**
   - Educating mortgage lenders and insurance professionals about Code Plus standards to facilitate favorable financing and insurance terms for compliant properties.

These education and training initiatives are crucial for building the capacity necessary to implement Code Plus standards effectively, regardless of whether the implementation approach is mandatory, voluntary, or phased.

Figure 12.2 From Code to Compliance: Enforcement Flow

Enforcement is a process, not a single step. Stronger building codes must be matched by investments in inspector training, product approval systems, and consistent oversight. When these elements align, communities achieve the intended outcome: resilient homes and reduced hurricane losses.

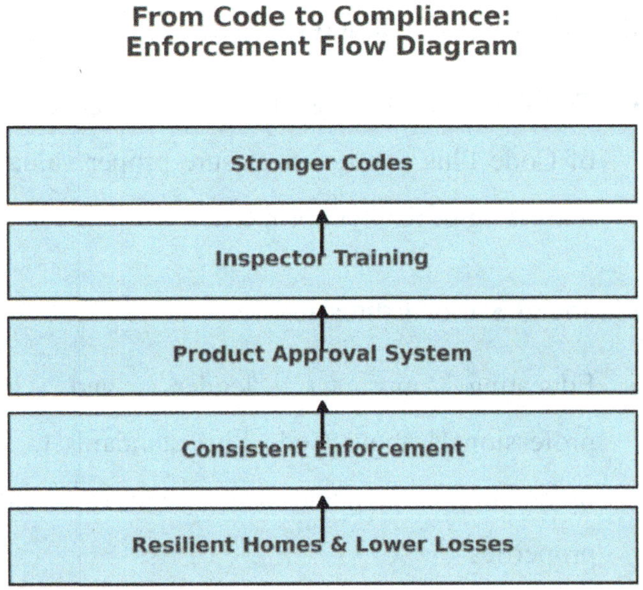

Enforcement Challenges and Strategies

Effective enforcement is the linchpin of successful Code Plus implementation. Even the strongest building standards are meaningless without consistent oversight to ensure compliance. Across jurisdictions, the challenge has been twofold: ensuring

capacity to enforce complex standards and overcoming **resistance** from stakeholders reluctant to adopt new practices.

Miami-Dade County provides one of the clearest examples. After Hurricane Andrew, the county's sweeping code overhaul introduced complex requirements for roof systems, structural connections, and impact-resistant openings. Initial enforcement proved uneven, with inspectors struggling to apply new rules consistently. Miami-Dade responded by **investing heavily in inspector training** and establishing a **rigorous product approval process** for windows, doors, roofing systems, and other critical components. These steps helped standardize compliance and ensured that approved materials met stringent performance criteria[221].

Florida's statewide building code faced an even greater enforcement challenge: ensuring uniform application across a large and diverse state. The state addressed this by creating the **Florida Building Commission**, a centralized authority responsible for code development, training, and oversight. The Commission also instituted **regular update cycles** to integrate post-disaster lessons and new research. These measures improved consistency across jurisdictions and gave stakeholders confidence that enforcement was both fair and adaptive[222].

---

[221] Miami-Dade inspector training and product approval system.

[222] Florida Building Commission, statewide enforcement, and update cycles.

Galveston, Texas shows how enforcement can be strengthened through partnership. Following Hurricane Ike, the city struggled with local enforcement capacity and industry pushback due to 20–30% higher costs in high-risk areas. The solution came through collaboration with Texas A&M University, which provided **technical training, simplified compliance checklists, and support for inspectors and builders**. By reducing uncertainty and equipping professionals with tools for success, Galveston improved compliance while easing industry resistance[223].

North Carolina's Fortified Homes Program highlights a different enforcement strategy: leveraging market incentives. Because the program is voluntary, compliance is ensured not by inspectors but by **insurance-linked verification** that qualifies homeowners for premium discounts. This approach sidesteps some enforcement burdens by embedding compliance into the insurance process itself[224].

Across these examples, a common theme emerges: **initial industry resistance** was universal, but it was overcome through a mix of strategies—phased implementation, third-party verification systems, investment in inspector training, and stakeholder engagement.

---

[223] Galveston partnership with Texas A&M for compliance training.
[224] North Carolina Fortified Homes Program insurance-linked verification.

Policy Takeaway: Enforcement is not an administrative afterthought; it is an essential investment. Without trained inspectors, robust oversight, and credible product approval systems, Code Plus cannot achieve its promised resilience. Policymakers should therefore allocate resources to enforcement capacity at the same priority level as technical standards themselves.

Adaptive Management and Continuous Improvement

Given the evolving nature of climate risks and building technologies, an adaptive management approach to Code Plus policies is crucial. This approach should include:

1. **Regular Review and Update Cycles:**
    - Establishing mandatory review cycles (e.g., every 3-5 years) to update Code Plus standards based on new research, post-disaster assessments, and climate projections.
    - Creating a dedicated committee for continuous code review with the authority to propose and implement targeted updates.

2. **Performance Monitoring:**

- Implementing systems to track the real-world performance of Code Plus buildings during hurricane events.
- Conducting post-disaster assessments to identify areas for improvement in Code Plus standards.

3. **Research and Development Support:**
    - Allocating funding for ongoing research into hurricane-resistant building technologies and practices.
    - Fostering partnerships between government agencies, academic institutions, and the private sector to drive innovation in resilient construction.
4. **Flexibility in Implementation:**
    - Building flexibility into Code Plus policies to allow for adjustments based on implementation experiences and new data.
    - Incorporating mechanisms for piloting new approaches or technologies within the Code Plus framework.

By adopting an adaptive management approach, policymakers can ensure that Code Plus standards remain effective and relevant in the face of changing climate conditions and evolving building practices.

Conclusion

The implementation of Code Plus standards represents a complex policy challenge that requires a multi-faceted approach. By carefully crafting regulatory frameworks, designing effective incentive structures, investing in education and training, addressing enforcement challenges, and adopting an adaptive management approach, policymakers can create an environment conducive to the widespread adoption of enhanced building standards.

The success of Code Plus implementation will ultimately depend on the ability to balance various stakeholder interests, navigate political and economic realities, and maintain a long-term perspective on community resilience. As we face increasing threats from hurricanes and other climate-related hazards, the thoughtful implementation of Code Plus standards offers a pathway to creating safer, more resilient coastal communities for generations to come.

Implementation is not hypothetical. Several states and localities have already tested versions of enhanced building standards. Their experiences—successes and setbacks alike—offer practical insights into what Florida can expect if Code Plus moves forward.

PART V: LESSON FROM THE FIELD

Chapter 13

Success Stories

Communities That Got It Right

Introduction

Theory and analysis provide the foundation, but real-world experience offers the proof. This section examines communities that have already implemented enhanced building standards, documenting their successes, challenges, and adaptations. From Miami-Dade's pioneering mandatory codes to North Carolina's market-based approach, these case studies reveal what works, what doesn't, and what Florida can learn as it considers expanding Code Plus standards statewide.

Case Studies: Success Stories of Code Plus Implementations

The implementation of enhanced building standards akin to Code Plus has been undertaken in various regions prone to hurricane risks. These real-world examples provide valuable insights into the practical applications, challenges, and benefits of such standards. By examining these case studies in depth, we can glean important lessons for future Code Plus implementations across different contexts and implementation approaches.

Miami-Dade County, Florida: Pioneering Stringent Building Codes

Miami-Dade County stands as a testament to the effectiveness of enhanced building standards in mitigating hurricane damage. In the wake of the devastating Hurricane Andrew in 1992, which caused over $25 billion in damage and destroyed more than 63,000 homes, the county took decisive action to overhaul its building codes.[225] The resulting standards, often referred to as the "Miami-Dade Code," went far beyond the existing state requirements and served as a precursor to many of the concepts now embodied in Code Plus.

1. **Implementation Approach:**

   The Miami-Dade Code represents a mandatory implementation approach. Following Hurricane Andrew, the county quickly adopted emergency building code changes, which were later formalized into comprehensive, legally binding standards. This approach ensured rapid and

---

[225] Blake, E. S., et al. (2011). The deadliest, costliest, and most intense United States tropical cyclones from 1851 to 2010 (and other frequently requested hurricane facts). NOAA Technical Memorandum NWS NHC-6.

widespread adoption of enhanced building practices across the county.

Key features of the Miami-Dade Code included:

- Stringent requirements for impact-resistant windows and doors
- Enhanced standards for roof coverings and attachments
- Improved requirements for structural connections, particularly between roofs and walls
- A rigorous product approval process for building materials and components

2. Economic Impact:

The implementation of these enhanced standards had significant economic implications:

- Initial Cost Increase: The new standards increased construction costs by an estimated 3-5% for most homes.[226] For a typical $300,000 home, this translated to an additional $9,000 to $15,000 in construction costs.

---

[226] Simmons, K. M., et al. (2018). Economic effectiveness of implementing a statewide building code: The case of Florida. Land Economics, 94(2), 155-174.

- Long-term Savings: However, these upfront costs were offset by substantial long-term savings. A study conducted by the Insurance Institute for Business and Home Safety found that homes built to the new standards after Hurricane Andrew experienced 60% fewer instances of water infiltration and 40% fewer instances of structural damage during subsequent hurricanes, compared to homes built prior to the new code.[227]
- Insurance Implications: The improved resilience of newer homes led to significant reductions in insurance premiums. By 2005, homeowners with houses built to the post-Andrew code were receiving insurance discounts of up to 40%.[228]

3. Policy Lessons:

The Miami-Dade case offers several crucial policy lessons:

- Rapid Response to Disaster: The county's quick action in the aftermath of Hurricane Andrew demonstrates the

---

[227] Insurance Institute for Business and Home Safety. (2007). Hurricane Wilma: Nature's Window into Florida's Wind Insurance Problem. IBHS.
[228] Florida Office of Insurance Regulation. (2006). An Analysis of Florida's Insurance Market: The Impact of Hurricane Damage and the State of the Insurance Market.

importance of leveraging post-disaster awareness to implement significant policy changes.

- Comprehensive Approach: The Miami-Dade Code addressed multiple aspects of building resilience, from structural integrity to opening protection, showcasing the importance of a holistic approach to enhanced standards.
- Product Approval Process: The establishment of a rigorous product approval system ensured that building materials and components met the enhanced standards, highlighting the importance of quality control in implementing Code Plus standards.
- Continuous Improvement: Miami-Dade has continued to refine and enhance its building code over time, demonstrating the value of an adaptive management approach to building standards.

4. Challenges and Solutions:

The implementation of the Miami-Dade Code was not without its challenges:

- Initial Resistance: The construction industry initially pushed back against the new standards, citing increased costs and concerns about the availability of approved materials.

- Solution: The county worked closely with manufacturers to develop compliant products and implemented a phased approach to allow the industry to adapt. Over time, as the benefits became apparent and economies of scale developed, resistance diminished.
- Enforcement Consistency: Ensuring consistent enforcement of the new, more complex standards across the county posed a significant challenge.
- Solution: Miami-Dade invested heavily in training for building inspectors and developed detailed guidelines to ensure uniform application of the new code.

5. Long-term Outcomes:

The long-term impact of the Miami-Dade Code has been substantial:

- Reduced Hurricane Damage: During Hurricane Wilma in 2005, homes built to the new standards fared significantly better than older structures. A study found that these homes experienced 70% less damage than pre-code homes.[229]

---

[229] Gurley, K., et al. (2006). Post 2004 Hurricane Field Survey of Residential Building Performance. Natural Hazards Review, 7(2), 29-44.

- Economic Resilience: The enhanced building standards have contributed to Miami-Dade's overall economic resilience. The county has seen faster recovery times and reduced economic disruption following recent hurricane events.
- Industry Adaptation: Over time, the construction industry in Miami-Dade has fully adapted to the enhanced standards, developing expertise that has positioned local firms as leaders in hurricane-resistant construction.

The Miami-Dade case illustrates the potential long-term benefits of mandatory Code Plus standards while also highlighting the importance of stakeholder engagement and flexible implementation strategies in overcoming initial obstacles.

North Carolina: The Fortified Homes Program

North Carolina's coast, with its exposure to Atlantic hurricanes, has been a testing ground for enhanced building standards through the Fortified Homes program. Developed by the Insurance Institute for Business & Home Safety (IBHS), this program offers a set of above-code construction standards that align closely with the principles of Code Plus.[230]

---

[230] Insurance Institute for Business and Home Safety. (2020). FORTIFIED Home™ Hurricane Standards. IBHS.

1. **Implementation Approach:**

The Fortified program in North Carolina represents a voluntary implementation approach, with elements of a phased strategy. Unlike the mandatory standards in Miami-Dade, North Carolina has opted for an incentive-based system to encourage adoption of enhanced building practices.

Key features of the Fortified program include:

- Three levels of certification: Bronze, Silver, and Gold, each providing increasingly comprehensive protection against hurricane forces
- Focus on critical areas such as roof performance, opening protection, and continuous load paths from roof to foundation
- Applicability to both new construction and retrofits of existing homes

2. **Economic Impact:**

The economic implications of the Fortified program in North Carolina have been significant:

- Initial Costs: The cost to build or retrofit to Fortified standards varies depending on the level of certification. On average, achieving Bronze level certification adds about 3% to construction costs, while Gold level can add up to 10%.[231]

- Insurance Incentives: In 2016, North Carolina passed legislation offering insurance premium discounts for homes built or retrofitted to Fortified standards. These discounts range from 5% to 20%, depending on the level of certification and location of the property.[232]
- Property Value Increase: A study by the University of Alabama found that Fortified homes in North Carolina commanded a 7% premium in resale value compared to similar, non-Fortified homes.[233]

3. Policy Lessons:

The North Carolina case offers valuable insights into voluntary implementation strategies:

- Tiered Approach: The three-level certification system allows homeowners to incrementally improve their home's resilience, making the adoption of enhanced

---

[231] Czajkowski, J., & Simmons, K. M. (2014). Convective storm vulnerability: Quantifying the role of effective and well-enforced building codes in minimizing Missouri hail property damage. Land Economics, 90(3), 482-508.

[232] North Carolina Department of Insurance. (2019). Insurance Premium Discounts for FORTIFIED Homes. NC DOI.

[233] Dumm, R. E., et al. (2011). The capitalization of building codes in house prices. The Journal of Real Estate Finance and Economics, 42(1), 30-50.

standards more accessible and appealing to a broader range of property owners.

- Legislative Support: The state's decision to mandate insurance discounts for Fortified homes demonstrates how policy can create economic incentives for voluntary adoption of enhanced standards.
- Public-Private Partnership: The collaboration between the state government, IBHS, and insurance companies showcases the potential of multi-stakeholder approaches in promoting resilient construction.

4. Challenges and Solutions:

The implementation of the Fortified program in North Carolina has faced several challenges:

- Awareness and Education: Initially, many homeowners and builders were unfamiliar with the Fortified standards and their benefits.
- Solution: IBHS and state agencies launched comprehensive education campaigns, including workshops for builders and real estate professionals, and public awareness initiatives for homeowners.
- Retrofit Costs: The cost of retrofitting existing homes to meet Fortified standards was a significant barrier for many homeowners.

- Solution: North Carolina implemented grant programs to assist homeowners with retrofit costs, particularly focusing on low-income households in high-risk areas.

5. Long-term Outcomes:

The Fortified program has shown promising results in North Carolina:

- Adoption Rates: By 2020, over 3,000 homes in North Carolina had achieved Fortified certification, with adoption rates accelerating each year.[234]
- Performance in Hurricanes: Following Hurricane Florence in 2018, a study of affected areas found that Fortified homes experienced significantly less damage than neighboring properties built to standard codes. Specifically, Fortified homes were 85% less likely to experience any damage to the roof cover.[235]
- Market Transformation: The success of the Fortified program has begun to influence broader building practices in North Carolina, with some local jurisdictions considering incorporating Fortified standards into their building codes.

---

[234] Insurance Institute for Business and Home Safety. (2021). FORTIFIED in Your State: North Carolina. IBHS.
[235] Simmons, K. M., et al. (2019). Effectiveness of a FORTIFIED Home™ Hurricane Standard. Weather, Climate, and Society, 11(4), 917-927.

The North Carolina case highlights the power of combining enhanced building standards with financial incentives. It also demonstrates the importance of creating a tiered system that allows homeowners to incrementally improve their home's resilience, making the adoption of enhanced standards more accessible and appealing to a broader range of property owners.

Texas Gulf Coast: Galveston's Post-Ike Building Code Reforms

The city of Galveston, Texas, provides an instructive example of implementing enhanced building standards in response to a catastrophic event. After Hurricane Ike devastated the island in 2008, causing over $29 billion in damage, Galveston undertook a comprehensive review and enhancement of its building codes.[236]

1. **Implementation Approach:**

   Galveston's approach represents a hybrid model, combining elements of mandatory implementation with a phased introduction of enhanced standards. The city implemented immediate changes to address critical vulnerabilities while setting a timeline for more comprehensive enhancements.

2. **Key features of Galveston's approach included:**

---

[236] Highfield, W. E., et al. (2014). Mitigation planning: Why hazard exposure, structural vulnerability, and social vulnerability matter. Journal of Planning Education and Research, 34(3), 287-300.

- Immediate mandatory elevation requirements for new construction and substantial renovations
- Phased introduction of enhanced wind resistance standards
- Creation of a "Coastal High Hazard Area" designation with stricter building requirements

3. Economic Impact:

The economic implications of Galveston's enhanced building standards have been multifaceted:

- Initial Cost Increase: The new standards, particularly the elevation requirements, increased construction costs by an estimated 20-30% for homes in high-risk areas.[237]
- Insurance Implications: Properties meeting the new standards have seen reductions in flood insurance premiums, with some homeowners reporting savings of up to 60%.[238]
- Property Values: Despite initial concerns, a study conducted five years after implementation found that

---

[237] Berke, P. R., et al. (2014). Adaptive planning for disaster recovery and resiliency: An evaluation of 87 local recovery plans in eight states. Journal of the American Planning Association, 80(4), 310-323.

[238] Federal Emergency Management Agency. (2018). Loss Avoidance Study: Galveston, Texas Regulatory Requirements for Building Elevation. FEMA.

properties built to the new standards commanded a 10-15% premium in the real estate market compared to similar pre-code properties.[239]

3. Policy Lessons:

Galveston's experience offers several important policy insights:

- Tailored Approach: The creation of the "Coastal High Hazard Area" demonstrates the value of tailoring enhanced standards to specific local conditions and risk profiles.
- Balancing Immediate Action and Long-term Planning: Galveston's approach of implementing critical changes immediately while phasing in more comprehensive standards over time offers a model for balancing urgency with practicality.
- Integration with Community Planning: The building code reforms were integrated into broader community resilience planning, including updates to zoning ordinances and infrastructure improvements.

---

[239] Botzen, W. J., et al. (2019). The benefits of natural flood insurance in a changing climate: Insights from a quasi-experimental study in Florida. Journal of Environmental Economics and Management, 95, 26-41.

4. Challenges and Solutions:

Galveston faced significant challenges in implementing its enhanced building standards:

- Economic Concerns: There was substantial worry about the impact of increased construction costs on the island's economy, which relies heavily on tourism and seasonal residences.
- Solution: The city adopted a phased implementation approach and worked closely with local builders and architects to develop cost-effective compliance strategies. They also implemented a public education campaign highlighting the long-term economic benefits of resilient construction.
- Technical Complexity: The new standards, particularly those related to wind resistance and flood-proofing, were technically complex and initially challenging for local builders to implement.
- Solution: Galveston partnered with Texas A&M University to provide technical training and support for local construction professionals. They also developed simplified guidance documents and checklists to aid in compliance.

5. Long-term Outcomes:

While it's still relatively early to fully assess the long-term impacts, initial results are promising:

- Improved Resilience: New construction in Galveston has demonstrated markedly improved resilience to subsequent storm events. During Hurricane Harvey in 2017, homes built to the new standards experienced significantly less damage than older structures.[240]
- Economic Recovery: Despite initial concerns, Galveston's construction industry has adapted to the new standards, and the city has seen a steady pace of new development and redevelopment.
- Community Resilience: The enhanced building standards, combined with other resilience measures, have contributed to an overall increase in community resilience. Galveston has seen improvements in its Community Rating System score, leading to community-wide flood insurance premium reductions.[241]

---

[240] Berke, P. R., et al. (2018). Evaluation of networks of plans and vulnerability to hazards and climate change: A resilience scorecard. Journal of the American Planning Association, 84(1), 45-58.

[241] Federal Emergency Management Agency. (2021). Community Rating System (CRS) Communities and their Classes. FEMA.

The Galveston case underscores the importance of tailoring enhanced building standards to local conditions and vulnerabilities. It also highlights the potential for such standards to be implemented successfully even in economically sensitive coastal communities, provided there is a thoughtful, phased approach and strong community engagement.

Florida's Statewide Building Code: A Model for Comprehensive Reform

While we've discussed Miami-Dade County's pioneering efforts, it's crucial to examine Florida's statewide adoption of enhanced building standards, which represents one of the most comprehensive and long-standing examples of Code Plus-style implementation in the United States.

1. **Implementation Approach:**

   Florida's approach represents a mandatory, statewide implementation of enhanced building standards. Following the devastation of Hurricane Andrew in 1992, the state embarked on a comprehensive overhaul of its building codes, culminating in the implementation of the Florida Building Code in 2002.

Key features of Florida's approach included:

- A unified, statewide code replacing the patchwork of local codes
- Enhanced wind resistance standards based on local risk levels
- Improved standards for impact resistance and water intrusion prevention
- Regular update cycles to incorporate new research and lessons from subsequent hurricanes

2. Economic Impact:

The economic implications of Florida's enhanced building code have been substantial and well-documented:

- Initial Cost Increase: The implementation of the new code increased construction costs by an estimated 1-3% for most areas, with higher increases in high-risk coastal zones.[242]
- Insurance Implications: A study by the Insurance Institute for Business & Home Safety found that insured loss costs were reduced by 72% for homes built

[242] Florida Building Commission. (2004). Economic Impact Study of Florida Building Code. Florida Department of Community Affairs.

after the implementation of the 2002 code, compared to homes built before 1995.[243]

- Broader Economic Benefits: Research by the Federal Alliance for Safe Homes estimated that the stronger building code will prevent $50 billion in damage from wind-related perils over a 50-year period.[244]

3. Policy Lessons:

Florida's statewide implementation offers several crucial policy insights:

- Importance of Statewide Consistency: The move to a unified state code ensured consistent application of enhanced standards across diverse jurisdictions.
- Adaptive Management: Florida's code includes provisions for regular updates, allowing for the incorporation of new research and lessons from hurricane events.
- Risk-Based Approach: The code tailors wind resistance requirements to local risk levels, demonstrating the importance of nuanced, location-specific standards.

---

[243] Insurance Institute for Business and Home Safety. (2015). Hurricane Charley: Lessons Learned in Building Performance. IBHS.
[244] Federal Alliance for Safe Homes. (2019). Building Codes Save: A Nationwide Study. FLASH.

4. Challenges and Solutions:

Florida faced significant challenges in implementing and maintaining its enhanced building code:

- Initial Industry Resistance: As with Miami-Dade, there was initial pushback from the construction industry due to concerns about increased costs and complexity.
- Solution: The state engaged in extensive stakeholder consultation and provided a transition period for industry adaptation. They also invested in comprehensive training programs for builders and inspectors.
- Enforcement Consistency: Ensuring uniform enforcement across a large, diverse state proved challenging.
- Solution: Florida established the Florida Building Commission to oversee code development and implementation. They also developed standardized training programs for building officials across the state.
- Political Pressure: Over time, there have been efforts to weaken the code or reduce its scope.
- Solution: Advocates for the enhanced code have consistently highlighted its proven benefits, both in terms of safety and long-term economic savings.

They've also worked to educate policymakers about the importance of maintaining strong standards.

5. Long-term Outcomes:

Florida's enhanced building code has demonstrated significant positive outcomes over nearly two decades:

- Reduced Hurricane Damage: Multiple studies have shown that homes built to the new code perform significantly better during hurricanes. For example, during Hurricane Charley in 2004, homes built to the new code experienced 40% less damage than older homes.[245]
- Insurance Market Stabilization: While Florida still faces challenges in its property insurance market, the enhanced building code has contributed to greater stability and has helped maintain insurance availability in high-risk areas.
- Economic Resilience: Florida's enhanced building standards have contributed to the state's overall economic resilience in the face of hurricane threats. The state has generally seen faster recovery times and

---

[245] Gurley, K., et al. (2006). Post 2004 Hurricane Field Survey of Residential Building Performance. Natural Hazards Review, 7(2), 29-44.

reduced economic disruption following recent hurricane events compared to pre-code patterns.

- Industry Adaptation and Innovation: Over time, Florida's construction industry has not only adapted to the enhanced standards but has become a leader in hurricane-resistant building practices. This has led to the development of new technologies and construction methods that have been adopted in other hurricane-prone regions.[246]
- Export of Expertise: Florida's experience with enhanced building standards has positioned the state as a global leader in hurricane-resistant construction. Florida-based architects, engineers, and construction firms have exported their expertise to other hurricane-prone regions around the world.[247]

6. Ongoing Challenges and Future Directions:

Despite its successes, Florida's enhanced building code continues to face challenges and areas for improvement:

---

[246] Mostafavi, N., & Inman, D. (2018). Improving the resilience of structures using adaptive building envelopes. Engineering Structures, 175, 876-888.
[247] Agarwal, J., & Blockley, D. (2007). Structural integrity: Hazard, vulnerability and risk. International Journal of Materials and Structural Integrity, 1(1-3), 117-127.

- Climate Change Adaptation: There is ongoing debate about how to incorporate future climate projections, particularly sea-level rise, into the building code.[248]
- Existing Building Stock: While new construction is more resilient, a significant portion of Florida's building stock predates the enhanced code. Developing effective strategies for retrofitting older buildings remains a challenge.[249]
- Balancing Costs and Benefits: As the code continues to evolve, there is constant tension between enhancing resilience and managing construction costs, particularly in the context of affordable housing.[250]
- Maintaining Political Will: Ensuring continued support for strong building standards requires ongoing education of policymakers and the public about the long-term benefits of these measures.[251]

---

248 Haasnoot, M., et al. (2013). Dynamic adaptive policy pathways: A method for crafting robust decisions for a deeply uncertain world. Global Environmental Change, 23(2), 485-498.

249 Peacock, W. G., et al. (2018). The adoption and implementation of hazard-resistant building codes. Natural Hazards Review, 19(4), 04018018.

250 Burby, R. J. (2006). Hurricane Katrina and the paradoxes of government disaster policy: Bringing about wise governmental decisions for hazardous areas. The Annals of the American Academy of Political and Social Science, 604(1), 171-191.

251 Berke, P., & Godschalk, D. (2009). Searching for the good plan: A meta-analysis of plan quality studies. Journal of Planning Literature, 23(3), 227-240.

Florida's statewide implementation of enhanced building standards serves as a model for comprehensive, long-term commitment to building resilience. Its successes and challenges offer valuable lessons for other regions considering similar large-scale implementations of Code Plus standards.

Chapter 14

Learning from Experience

Comparative Analysis and Best Practices

Comparative Analysis of Case Studies

Examining these diverse case studies – Miami-Dade County, North Carolina's Fortified Homes Program, Galveston's post-Ike reforms, and Florida's statewide code – provides valuable insights into the various approaches to implementing enhanced building standards:

1. **Implementation Approaches:**
   - Mandatory vs. Voluntary: Miami-Dade and Florida represent mandatory approaches, while North Carolina's Fortified program is voluntary. Galveston used a hybrid approach. The mandatory approaches ensured widespread adoption but faced more initial resistance, while the voluntary approach in North Carolina allowed for more flexibility but resulted in slower adoption rates.

- Geographic Scope: The cases range from city-level (Galveston) to county-level (Miami-Dade) to state-wide (Florida) implementations, illustrating how enhanced standards can be tailored to different scales of governance.
- Timing: While Miami-Dade and Florida implemented changes relatively quickly after Hurricane Andrew, Galveston's approach was more gradual. This highlights the trade-offs between rapid implementation and allowing time for industry adaptation.

2. **Economic Impacts:**

- Initial Costs: All cases saw increases in initial construction costs, ranging from 1-3% in some areas of Florida to 20-30% in high-risk areas of Galveston. However, the long-term benefits consistently outweighed these upfront costs.
- Insurance Effects: All cases demonstrated significant positive impacts on insurance, including premium reductions and increased availability of coverage in high-risk areas.
- Property Values: In North Carolina and Galveston, homes built to enhanced standards commanded price

premiums in the real estate market, suggesting that buyers value these resilience features.

3. **Policy Strategies:**

   - Incentives: North Carolina's use of insurance premium discounts as an incentive for voluntary adoption stands out as a particularly effective strategy.

   - Phased Implementation: Galveston's phased approach offers a model for balancing immediate needs with long-term goals.

   - Continuous Improvement: Florida's regular code update cycle demonstrates the importance of adaptive management in maintaining effective standards over time.

4. **Challenges and Solutions:**

   - Industry Resistance: All cases faced initial pushback from the construction industry. Successful strategies to overcome this included stakeholder engagement, phased implementation, and investment in training and education.

   - Enforcement: Ensuring consistent enforcement was a common challenge, addressed through training programs, clear guidelines, and in some cases, third-party verification systems.

- Public Awareness: All cases highlighted the importance of public education to build support for enhanced standards and ensure compliance.

5. **Long-term Outcomes:**

- Damage Reduction: All cases demonstrated significant reductions in hurricane damage for buildings constructed to enhanced standards.
- Economic Resilience: The case studies consistently showed that regions with enhanced building standards experienced faster recovery and reduced economic disruption following hurricane events.
- Industry Transformation: Over time, the construction industry in these regions adapted to and even embraced the enhanced standards, often becoming leaders in resilient building practices.

Conclusion

These case studies collectively demonstrate the feasibility and benefits of implementing Code Plus-like standards across diverse contexts. They reveal common themes – the importance of stakeholder engagement, the value of integrating financial incentives, and the need for flexible, context-sensitive implementation strategies.

Moreover, these examples provide tangible evidence of the long-term benefits of enhanced building standards in terms of reduced damage, improved community resilience, and potential economic advantages through reduced insurance costs and faster post-disaster recovery.

The experiences of Miami-Dade County, North Carolina, Galveston, and the state of Florida offer valuable lessons for other regions considering the implementation of Code Plus standards. They highlight the importance of tailoring approaches to local conditions, the power of combining regulatory measures with economic incentives, and the need for ongoing adaptation and improvement of standards over time.

As we consider the broader implementation of Code Plus standards, these case studies offer not just inspiration but practical guidance. They show that with careful planning, community engagement, and a commitment to long-term resilience, it is possible to significantly enhance the hurricane resistance of our built environment, creating safer and more sustainable coastal communities for generations to come.

The case studies provide evidence from the present, but resilience is a moving target. Climate change, new technologies, and shifting demographics will shape tomorrow's risks. The following section looks ahead, positioning Code Plus within a broader horizon of adaptation and innovation.

PART VI: THE FUTURE OF RESILIENCE

Chapter 15

Tomorrow's Challenges
Climate Change and Evolving Threats

Future Perspectives and Emerging Trends

As we look to the future of Code Plus standards and hurricane-resistant construction, several key trends and emerging technologies promise to shape the landscape of building resilience. These developments not only offer the potential for even more effective protection against hurricane damage but also present new challenges and opportunities for policymakers, builders, and homeowners. This section explores the cutting-edge developments that are likely to influence the evolution of Code Plus standards in the coming years.

Climate Change Implications for Building Codes

The specter of climate change looms large over any discussion of future hurricane resilience. As global temperatures rise, climate scientists project changes in hurricane patterns that could have significant implications for building standards. The

Intergovernmental Panel on Climate Change (IPCC) suggests that while the overall frequency of hurricanes may not increase, the intensity of these storms is likely to grow, with more Category 4 and 5 hurricanes expected in the coming decades.[466]

1. **Projected Changes in Hurricane Patterns:**

Climate models predict several key changes in hurricane behavior that will directly impact building design requirements:

- Increased Wind Speeds: Maximum wind speeds in the most intense hurricanes are projected to increase by 2-11% by 2100.[467] This will necessitate more robust wind resistance measures in future Code Plus standards.
- Higher Rainfall Intensity: Warming temperatures are expected to increase the water-holding capacity of the atmosphere, leading to more intense rainfall during hurricanes. Some models project a 10-15% increase in rainfall rates within 100 km of the storm center.[468] This trend will require enhanced water intrusion prevention measures and improved drainage systems in Code Plus designs.
- Slower Storm Movement: Recent research indicates that hurricane translation speeds have decreased by about 10% since the mid-20th century, a trend that may

continue with further warming.[469] Slower-moving storms can lead to prolonged wind and rain exposure, potentially necessitating even more stringent durability requirements in Code Plus standards.

- Sea Level Rise: Global sea levels are projected to rise by 0.43-0.84 meters by 2100 under a high emissions scenario.[470] This will exacerbate storm surge risks, potentially requiring more extensive elevation requirements and flood-resistant design features in coastal Code Plus standards.

2. Implications for Code Plus Standards:

These projected changes in hurricane behavior will necessitate several adaptations in Code Plus standards:

- Dynamic Wind Load Calculations: Future Code Plus standards may need to incorporate more dynamic wind load calculations that account for potential increases in maximum wind speeds over a building's lifetime.
- Enhanced Water Management: Given projections for increased rainfall intensity, Code Plus standards will likely place even greater emphasis on robust water management systems, including improved roof drainage, enhanced waterproofing, and potentially the integration of green infrastructure solutions.

- Durability Under Prolonged Exposure: With the potential for slower-moving storms, Code Plus standards may need to consider the ability of materials and systems to withstand prolonged exposure to hurricane conditions, beyond the typical duration considered in current standards.
- Adaptive Design Approaches: To address the uncertainty inherent in long-term climate projections, future Code Plus standards may incorporate more flexible, adaptive design approaches. This could include provisions for easier future upgrades or the use of modular systems that can be enhanced as risks increase over time.

3. Challenges in Incorporating Climate Projections:

Integrating climate change projections into Code Plus standards presents several challenges:

- Uncertainty in Long-term Projections: While there is high confidence in the overall trends of climate change, precise local-scale projections remain challenging. This uncertainty makes it difficult to establish specific, quantifiable standards for future conditions.
- Balancing Preparedness and Practicality: There's a risk of overbuilding based on worst-case scenarios, which

could unnecessarily increase construction costs. Finding the right balance between preparedness and practical, cost-effective solutions will be crucial.

- Timeframes for Building Standards vs. Climate Change: Building codes typically operate on shorter update cycles (e.g., 3-6 years) compared to the longer-term projections used in climate models. Aligning these different timeframes in a meaningful way presents a significant challenge.

To address these challenges, some researchers propose the concept of "anticipatory design," where buildings are constructed not just to withstand current threats, but to adapt to evolving risks over their lifespan.[471] This approach could involve:

- Designing core building systems to higher standards than currently required, anticipating future increases in risk.
- Incorporating flexibility into designs to allow for easier future upgrades or enhancements.
- Using scenario-based design approaches that consider multiple possible future climate conditions.

Technological Innovations in Hurricane-Resistant Construction

Rapid advancements in materials science and construction technology offer exciting possibilities for enhancing hurricane resilience beyond current Code Plus standards. These innovations have the potential to not only improve performance but also to make Code Plus-compliant construction more cost-effective and widely accessible.

1. Advanced Materials:

Emerging materials with enhanced properties are poised to revolutionize hurricane-resistant construction:

- Self-Healing Concrete: Researchers at the University of Miami are developing a "self-healing" concrete that can automatically repair small cracks, potentially reducing water intrusion during hurricanes. This technology uses bacteria embedded in the concrete that activate when exposed to water, producing limestone to fill in cracks.[472]
- Ultra-High-Performance Concrete (UHPC): This material offers significantly higher strength and durability compared to traditional concrete, with some formulations achieving compressive strengths over 150 MPa. Its use in critical structural elements could dramatically enhance a building's ability to withstand extreme wind and debris impacts.[473]

- Advanced Polymer Composites: New polymer composites, such as fiber-reinforced polymers (FRP), offer high strength-to-weight ratios and excellent corrosion resistance. These materials could be particularly useful in coastal environments where salt corrosion is a concern.[474]
- Aerogel Insulation: This ultra-lightweight material provides superior thermal insulation while also offering excellent water resistance. When used in exterior walls, aerogel insulation could significantly reduce both energy costs and the risk of water damage during hurricanes.[475]

2. Smart Building Technologies:

The integration of smart technologies into building design offers new possibilities for enhancing hurricane resilience:

- Structural Health Monitoring Systems: Advanced sensor networks can provide real-time data on a building's structural integrity before, during, and after a hurricane event. These systems can alert occupants or maintenance teams to potential issues, allowing for proactive interventions.[476]
- Automated Hurricane Shutters: Smart shutter systems that can automatically deploy based on weather data or

remote commands could provide more reliable protection against wind and debris impacts.

- Smart Water Management: Intelligent water detection and management systems can help mitigate water intrusion damage by quickly identifying leaks and automatically shutting off water supplies in affected areas.

3. Advanced Design and Construction Techniques:

Innovations in design and construction methods are also contributing to enhanced hurricane resilience:

- 3D Printing in Construction: Large-scale 3D printing of building components or entire structures could allow for more complex, optimized designs that are difficult or cost-prohibitive to achieve with traditional construction methods. Some researchers envision 3D-printed structures with integrated wind and water resistance features that go beyond current Code Plus capabilities.[477]
- Modular and Prefabricated Construction: Advanced prefabrication techniques can allow for higher quality control in the manufacturing of critical building components. This approach could lead to more

consistent implementation of Code Plus features and potentially reduce on-site construction errors.

- Computational Design Optimization: Advanced computational tools, including artificial intelligence and machine learning algorithms, are enabling more sophisticated optimization of building designs for hurricane resistance. These tools can analyze countless design variations to find optimal solutions that balance performance, cost, and constructability.[478]

4. Dynamic Facade Systems:

Emerging technologies in building envelope design offer new possibilities for adaptive hurricane resistance:

- Morphing Facades: Researchers are developing dynamic facade systems that can adapt to changing wind conditions. These systems use sensors and actuators to adjust the building's exterior in real-time, potentially reducing wind loads during hurricane events.[479]

- Smart Windows: Advanced glazing technologies, such as electrochromic or thermochromic materials, could enhance both energy efficiency and storm resistance by dynamically adjusting their properties in response to environmental conditions.

5. **Energy Resilience Technologies:**

Innovations in energy systems can enhance a building's ability to maintain critical functions during and after hurricane events:

- Integrated Renewable Energy Systems: Advanced integration of solar panels, small-scale wind turbines, and energy storage systems can provide crucial power generation capacity in the aftermath of storms. Innovative mounting systems are being developed that allow these systems to withstand hurricane-force winds.[480]
- Microgrid Technologies: The development of smart microgrid systems can allow buildings or communities to isolate from the main power grid during outages, maintaining power supply through a combination of local generation and storage.

While these technological innovations offer exciting possibilities for enhancing hurricane resilience, their integration into Code Plus standards will require careful consideration. Factors such as long-term durability, cost-effectiveness, and ease of implementation will need to be thoroughly evaluated before these technologies can be widely adopted in building codes.

Chapter 16

Innovation at the Edge

Emerging Technologies and Next-Generation Solutions

Evolving Regulatory Approaches

As our understanding of hurricane risks and building performance improves, regulatory approaches to Code Plus standards are likely to evolve. There's a growing recognition that prescriptive, one-size-fits-all standards may not always lead to optimal outcomes, particularly given the diversity of building types and local conditions in hurricane-prone regions.

1. **Performance-Based Codes:**

   Performance-based building codes, which specify desired outcomes rather than prescribing specific methods, are gaining traction in the field of hurricane-resistant design. This approach allows for more flexibility and innovation in meeting resilience goals.[252]

---

[252] Meacham, B. J. (2010). Performance-based building regulatory systems: principles and experiences. Inter-jurisdictional Regulatory Collaboration Committee.

Key features of performance-based codes include:

- Clear Performance Objectives: Instead of prescribing specific construction methods, these codes set clear performance targets, such as maintaining structural integrity under defined wind loads or preventing water intrusion during specified rainfall intensities.
- Flexibility in Solutions: Designers and builders have more freedom to innovate and find cost-effective solutions that meet the performance criteria.
- Site-Specific Optimization: Performance-based codes allow for more nuanced, site-specific designs that can better account for local conditions and risks.

Challenges in implementing performance-based codes include:

- Complexity in Verification: Ensuring compliance with performance-based standards often requires more sophisticated analysis and testing methods.
- Expertise Requirements: Building officials and designers need a higher level of expertise to effectively implement and enforce performance-based codes.
- Potential for Variability: Without prescriptive standards, there's a risk of greater variability in building performance across different projects.

2. Adaptive Codes:

The concept of "adaptive codes" that can be quickly updated in response to new data or changing conditions is gaining attention. This approach aims to make building codes more responsive to emerging threats and new knowledge.[253]

Key aspects of adaptive codes include:

- Regular Review Cycles: Mandating more frequent reviews and updates of building codes, potentially on an annual or biennial basis.
- Incorporation of Real-Time Data: Utilizing data from recent hurricane events and ongoing climate research to inform rapid code updates.
- Flexible Implementation: Allowing for quicker adoption of critical updates without waiting for full code revision cycles.

Challenges in implementing adaptive codes include:

- Industry Adaptation: Frequent changes can be challenging for the construction industry to keep up with and implement effectively.

---

[253] Haasnoot, M., et al. (2013). Dynamic adaptive policy pathways: A method for crafting robust decisions for a deeply uncertain world. Global Environmental Change, 23(2), 485-498.

- Enforcement Complexity: Building officials need to be continually trained on new requirements, which can strain resources in many jurisdictions.
- Potential for Inconsistency: Rapid changes could lead to inconsistencies in building standards across projects started at different times.

3. **Risk-Informed Regulations:**

There's a growing trend towards more nuanced, risk-informed approaches to building regulations. This involves tailoring code requirements based on detailed risk assessments that consider both the likelihood and potential consequences of different hazard scenarios.[254]

Key features of risk-informed regulations include:

- Graduated Requirements: Implementing stricter standards in higher-risk areas while allowing more flexibility in lower-risk zones.
- Multi-Hazard Approach: Considering the interplay of multiple hazards (e.g., wind, flooding, and debris impact) in determining building requirements.

---

[254] Keenan, J. M. (2018). Climate adaptation finance and investment in California. Routledge.

- Cost-Benefit Considerations: Explicitly factoring in the economic implications of different code provisions to ensure that requirements are both effective and economically viable.

Challenges in implementing risk-informed regulations include:

- Data Requirements: Effective risk-informed approaches require extensive, up-to-date data on local hazards and vulnerabilities.
- Complexity in Administration: Implementing and enforcing variable standards based on risk can be administratively complex.
- Public Understanding: Communicating the rationale for different standards in different areas can be challenging and may raise equity concerns.

Integration with Other Building Performance Goals

The future of Code Plus standards is likely to see increased integration with other building performance objectives, particularly energy efficiency and sustainability. This holistic approach recognizes that resilience cannot be considered in isolation from other crucial aspects of building design and operation.

1. **Synergies with Energy Efficiency:**

Many hurricane-resilient design features can also contribute to improved energy performance. Future Code Plus standards are likely to emphasize these synergies:

- High-Performance Building Envelopes: Enhanced insulation and air sealing required for hurricane resistance can also significantly improve a building's thermal performance.
- Impact-Resistant Windows: Many impact-resistant glazing systems also offer superior thermal insulation properties, contributing to both resilience and energy efficiency.
- Cool Roofing: Highly reflective and durable roofing materials that resist wind damage can also reduce cooling loads in hot climates.

2. **Incorporation of Sustainability Principles:**

Future iterations of Code Plus standards may increasingly incorporate broader sustainability considerations:

- Material Selection: Emphasis on durable, low-maintenance materials that not only enhance resilience but also reduce the building's life-cycle environmental impact.

- Water Conservation: Integration of rainwater harvesting and greywater systems that serve both sustainability goals and provide emergency water supplies during post-hurricane recovery periods.
- Renewable Energy Integration: Incorporation of hurricane-resistant solar panel mounting systems and other renewable energy technologies to enhance both resilience and sustainability.

3. Holistic Resilience Approaches:

The concept of "passive survivability" – a building's ability to maintain critical life-support conditions during extended power outages or loss of heating fuel or water – is gaining traction. This approach combines hurricane resilience with energy efficiency and passive design strategies.[255]

Key features of passive survivability include:

- Thermal Resilience: Designing building envelopes to maintain habitable interior temperatures without active heating or cooling systems.

---

[255] Wilson, A. (2006). Passive survivability: A new design criterion for buildings. Environmental Building News, 15(5), 1-8.

- Daylighting: Maximizing natural light to reduce dependence on electrical lighting systems during power outages.
- Natural Ventilation: Incorporating design features that allow for effective passive ventilation, crucial for comfort and air quality during extended power losses.

Future Challenges and Opportunities

As we look ahead, several key challenges and opportunities are likely to shape the evolution of Code Plus standards:

1. **Balancing Costs and Benefits:**
    - Challenge: As Code Plus standards become more comprehensive and sophisticated, there's a risk of significantly increasing construction costs, potentially impacting housing affordability.
    - Opportunity: Continued research and innovation in materials and construction techniques could help mitigate cost increases. Additionally, more sophisticated economic modeling of long-term benefits could help justify initial investments.

2. **Addressing Existing Building Stock:**
    - Challenge: While new construction can incorporate the latest Code Plus standards, the vast majority of

buildings in hurricane-prone areas were constructed to older, less stringent codes.

- Opportunity: Development of cost-effective retrofit strategies and incentive programs could help improve the resilience of existing buildings. Emerging technologies like easy-to-install impact-resistant window films or roof strengthening systems could play a crucial role.

3. **Climate Change Uncertainty:**

- Challenge: The uncertainty in long-term climate projections makes it difficult to set specific, quantifiable standards for future conditions.

- Opportunity: Adaptive design approaches and flexible building systems that can be upgraded over time could help address this uncertainty. Additionally, advances in climate modeling and risk assessment techniques could improve our ability to project future hazards.

4. **Workforce Development:**

- Challenge: Implementing increasingly complex Code Plus standards requires a highly skilled workforce, from designers and engineers to construction workers and building inspectors.

- Opportunity: Investment in education and training programs could not only address this challenge but also create new job opportunities in the field of resilient construction.

5. **Public Awareness and Support:**
   - Challenge: Maintaining public and political support for stringent building standards can be difficult, especially in the absence of recent major hurricane events.
   - Opportunity: Advanced visualization technologies and public education campaigns could help communicate the importance of Code Plus standards more effectively. Virtual reality simulations of hurricane impacts on different building types, for example, could be a powerful educational tool.

6. **Harnessing Big Data and AI:**
   - Challenge: The increasing complexity of hurricane risk assessment and building performance optimization requires processing and analyzing vast amounts of data.
   - Opportunity: Advances in big data analytics and artificial intelligence could revolutionize how we design, construct, and evaluate hurricane-resistant buildings. AI-driven design tools could optimize building configurations for both performance and cost-

effectiveness, while machine learning algorithms could improve our ability to predict and mitigate hurricane impacts.

Conclusion

The future of Code Plus standards is one of both exciting possibilities and significant challenges. As we face the dual pressures of climate change and rapid technological advancement, the field of hurricane-resistant construction is likely to see dramatic innovations in the coming decades.

From climate-adaptive design approaches and cutting-edge materials to smart building technologies and performance-based regulations, the tools and strategies available for enhancing hurricane resilience are expanding rapidly. At the same time, the integration of resilience with other crucial building performance goals, particularly energy efficiency and sustainability, promises to create structures that are not only safer but also more environmentally responsible and economically efficient over their lifecycle.

However, realizing the full potential of these advancements will require overcoming significant challenges. Balancing the costs of enhanced standards with affordability concerns, addressing the vulnerability of existing building stock, and navigating the uncertainties of climate change will all require careful consideration and innovative solutions.

Ultimately, the evolution of Code Plus standards will need to be a collaborative effort, involving policymakers, researchers, industry professionals, and community stakeholders. By embracing emerging technologies, adapting regulatory approaches, and maintaining a commitment to continuous improvement, we can work towards a future where our built environment is truly resilient in the face of increasing hurricane threats.

As we move forward, it will be crucial to maintain flexibility in our approaches, continually incorporate new knowledge and technologies, and always keep sight of the ultimate goal: creating safer, more resilient communities that can thrive in an uncertain future.

Taken together, the evidence—historical, scientific, economic, and practical—points to a single conclusion: Code Plus is both necessary and feasible. The final section distills these insights into concrete recommendations tailored for policymakers, insurers, and builders.

These emerging technologies and evolving approaches offer tremendous promise for enhancing hurricane resilience beyond what we can achieve today. But promise alone doesn't protect communities. The path forward requires immediate action based on proven strategies, even as we continue developing tomorrow's innovations. Our final chapter synthesizes everything we've learned into a clear roadmap for coastal communities ready to act.

CONCLUSION

Chapter 17

The Path Forward

A Call to Action for Coastal Communities

Conclusions and Recommended Action Steps

The evidence is clear: Code Plus delivers positive returns for homeowners, insurers, and communities. The question is no longer *whether* to adopt these standards, but *how* to accelerate adoption while addressing equity and enforcement challenges.

Action Step 1. Make Code Plus the Standard, Not the Exception

- Transition from voluntary incentives to phased mandatory adoption in high-risk areas.
- Establish a clear timeline (e.g., five years) for full integration into the Florida Building Code.

Action Step 2. Pair Standards with Equity Mechanisms

- Provide **grants, tax credits, and low-interest loans** to offset upfront costs for lower- and middle-income households.
- Expand insurance-linked incentives so savings are immediate, not deferred.

Action Step 3. Invest in Enforcement Capacity

- Fund inspector training and certification programs statewide.
- Strengthen product approval systems for windows, doors, and roofing to ensure quality compliance.
- Support local governments with resources for consistent enforcement.

Action Step 4. Align Incentives Across Sectors

- Require insurers to recognize and reward Code Plus adoption with substantial premium reductions.
- Encourage mortgage lenders to integrate resilience ratings into underwriting.
- Use state bonding authority or resilience bonds to finance upfront implementation.

Action Step 5. Institutionalize Continuous Improvement

- Mandate regular review cycles to incorporate new science, materials, and lessons from future storms.
- Establish a public–private resilience council to advise on long-term code evolution.
- Leverage new technologies, including AI-driven risk models, to anticipate vulnerabilities before disaster strikes.

Closing Note

Florida has historically strengthened its building codes only after disaster. Code Plus offers the chance to reverse that cycle—acting **before** the next storm, not after. By following these steps, policymakers can ensure that resilience becomes the foundation of Florida's economic stability, not a fragile afterthought.

Appendix A

The following is a comprehensive list of sources referenced in this report. They include a mix of academic journal articles, government reports, book, and institutional publications:

Aerts, J. C., & Botzen, W. W. (2011). Climate change impacts on pricing long-term flood insurance: A comprehensive study for the Netherlands. Global Environmental Change, 21(3), 1045-1060.

Agarwal, J., & Blockley, D. (2007). Structural integrity: Hazard, vulnerability and risk. International Journal of Materials and Structural Integrity, 1(1-3), 117-127.

Aktas, C. B., & Bilec, M. M. (2012). Impact of lifetime on US residential building LCA results. The International Journal of Life Cycle Assessment, 17(3), 337-349.

American Society of Civil Engineers. (2016). Minimum Design Loads and Associated Criteria for Buildings and Other Structures (ASCE/SEI 7-16).

Amini, M., & van de Lindt, J. (2014). Quantitative insight into rational tornado design wind speeds for residential wood-frame structures using fragility approach. Journal of Structural Engineering, 140(7), 04014033.

Bagstad, K. J., et al. (2007). Taxes, subsidies, and insurance as drivers of United States coastal development. Ecological Economics, 63(2-3), 285-298.

Baheru, T., et al. (2015). Wind-driven rain intrusion through deficient building envelope systems. Building and Environment, 94, 126-141.

Barnes, J. (1998). Florida's Hurricane History. University of North Carolina Press.

Berg, R., & Reinhart, B. J. (2023). Hurricane Ian. National Hurricane Center Tropical Cyclone Report.

Berke, P., & Godschalk, D. (2009). Searching for the good plan: A meta-analysis of plan quality studies. Journal of Planning Literature, 23(3), 227-240.

Berke, P. R., et al. (2014). Adaptive planning for disaster recovery and resiliency: An evaluation of 87 local recovery plans in eight states. Journal of the American Planning Association, 80(4), 310-323.

Berke, P. R., et al. (2018). Evaluation of networks of plans and vulnerability to hazards and climate change: A resilience scorecard. Journal of the American Planning Association, 84(1), 45-58.

Beven II, J. L., et al. (2019). Hurricane Michael. National Hurricane Center Tropical Cyclone Report.

Biggs, R., et al. (2012). Toward principles for enhancing the resilience of ecosystem services. Annual Review of Environment and Resources, 37, 421-448.

Bitsuamlak, G. T., et al. (2009). Computational assessment of blockage and wind simulator proximity effects for a new full-scale testing facility. Wind and Structures, 12(1), 21-36.

Blake, E. S., et al. (2011). The deadliest, costliest, and most intense United States tropical cyclones from 1851 to 2010 (and other frequently requested hurricane facts). NOAA Technical Memorandum NWS NHC-6.

Born, P. H., & Klimaszewski-Blettner, B. (2013). Should I stay or should I go? The impact of natural disasters and regulation on U.S. property insurers' supply decisions. Journal of Risk and Insurance, 80(1), 1-36.

Born, P. H., & Viscusi, W. K. (2006). The catastrophic effects of natural disasters on insurance markets. Journal of Risk and Uncertainty, 33(1-2), 55-72.

Bosher, L., et al. (2007). Integrating disaster risk management into construction: a UK perspective. Building Research & Information, 35(2), 163-177.

Botzen, W. J., et al. (2019). The benefits of natural flood insurance in a changing climate: Insights from a quasi-experimental study in Florida. Journal of Environmental Economics and Management, 95, 26-41.

Brown, R. E. (2009). Electric power distribution reliability (2nd ed.). CRC Press.

Bruneau, M., et al. (2003). A framework to quantitatively assess and enhance the seismic resilience of communities. Earthquake Spectra, 19(4), 733-752.

Burby, R. J. (2006). Hurricane Katrina and the paradoxes of government disaster policy: Bringing about wise governmental decisions for hazardous areas. The Annals of the American Academy of Political and Social Science, 604(1), 171-191.

California Energy Commission. (2021). California Energy Efficiency: Time-Dependent Valuation Overview.

Cangialosi, J. P., et al. (2018). Hurricane Irma. National Hurricane Center Tropical Cyclone Report.

Crossett, K. M., et al. (2013). National coastal population report: Population trends from 1970 to 2020. NOAA State of the Coast Report Series, US Department of Commerce, Washington.

Cutter, S. L., et al. (2008). A place-based model for understanding community resilience to natural disasters. Global Environmental Change, 18(4), 598-606.

Czajkowski, J., & Simmons, K. M. (2014). Convective storm vulnerability: Quantifying the role of effective and well-enforced building codes in minimizing Missouri hail property damage. Land Economics, 90(3), 482-508.

Datin, P. L., et al. (2011). Wind-induced internal pressures in hip roofs. Journal of Wind Engineering and Industrial Aerodynamics, 99(5), 568-576.

Dean, R. G., & Dalrymple, R. A. (2004). Coastal Processes with Engineering Applications. Cambridge University Press.

Dehring, C. A., & Halek, M. (2013). Coastal building codes and hurricane damage. Land Economics, 89(4), 597-613.

Dixon, C. R., et al. (2014). Impact of enhanced building codes on future wind loss reduction for residential structures in the United States. Frontiers in Built Environment, 3, 73.

Dumm, R. E., et al. (2011). The capitalization of building codes in house prices. The Journal of Real Estate Finance and Economics, 42(1), 30-50.

Dunn, G. E., & Miller, B. I. (1964). Atlantic hurricanes. Louisiana State University Press.

Duryea, M. L., et al. (2007). Hurricanes and the urban forest: II. Effects on tropical and subtropical tree species. Arboriculture and Urban Forestry, 33(2), 98-112.

Eagle, S. J. (2013). Coastal Construction Takings After Hurricane Sandy. Probate & Property, 27(5), 46-51.

Ellingwood, B. R., & Wen, Y. K. (2005). Risk-benefit-based design decisions for low-probability/high consequence earthquake events in mid-America. Progress in Structural Engineering and Materials, 7(2), 56-70.

Emanuel, K. (2017). Assessing the present and future probability of Hurricane Harvey's rainfall. Proceedings of the National Academy of Sciences, 114(48), 12681-12684.

Federal Alliance for Safe Homes. (2019). Building Codes Save: A Nationwide Study. FLASH.

Federal Emergency Management Agency. (2005). Mitigation Assessment Team Report: Hurricane Frances in Florida. FEMA 487.

Federal Emergency Management Agency. (2006). Hurricane Ivan in Alabama and Florida: Observations, Recommendations, and Technical Guidance. FEMA 489.

Federal Emergency Management Agency. (2006). Hurricane Wilma in Florida: Observations, Recommendations, and Technical Guidance. FEMA 549.

Federal Emergency Management Agency. (2011). Coastal Construction Manual: Principles and Practices of Planning, Siting, Designing, Constructing, and Maintaining Residential Buildings in Coastal Areas (4th ed.). FEMA P-55.

Federal Emergency Management Agency. (2018). Loss Avoidance Study: Galveston, Texas Regulatory Requirements for Building Elevation. FEMA.

Federal Emergency Management Agency. (2018). Mitigation Assessment Team Report: Hurricanes Irma and Maria in Puerto Rico. FEMA P-2020.

Federal Emergency Management Agency. (2021). Community Rating System (CRS) Communities and their Classes. FEMA.

Florida Building Commission. (2002). Florida Building Code. International Code Council.

Florida Building Commission. (2004). Economic Impact Study of Florida Building Code. Florida Department of Community Affairs.

Florida Building Commission. (2007). Florida Building Code 2007. International Code Council.

Florida Building Commission. (2010). Florida Building Code 2010. International Code Council.

Florida Building Commission. (2014). Florida Building Code 5th Edition (2014). International Code Council.

Florida Building Commission. (2017). Florida Building Code 6th Edition (2017). International Code Council.

Florida Building Commission. (2020). Florida Building Code 7th Edition (2020). International Code Council.

Florida Department of Community Affairs. (2002). Florida Building Code: Building. International Code Council.

Florida Department of Community Affairs. (2005). Florida Building Code 2004. International Code Council.

Florida Department of Community Affairs. (2005). Hurricane Charley in Florida: Building Performance Observations, Recommendations, and Technical Guidance.

Florida Office of Insurance Regulation. (2006). An Analysis of Florida's Insurance Market: The Impact of Hurricane Damage and the State of the Insurance Market.

Florida Office of Insurance Regulation. (2021). Annual Report on the State of the Florida Insurance Market.

Florida Statutes. (1998). Building Construction Standards. Chapter 553.

Fothergill, A., & Peek, L. A. (2004). Poverty and disasters in the United States: A review of recent sociological findings. Natural Hazards, 32(1), 89-110.

Gavanski, E., & Kopp, G. A. (2011). Examination of load resistance in window glass design. Journal of Architectural Engineering, 17(1), 42-50.

Godschalk, D. R., et al. (2003). Public participation in natural hazard mitigation policy formation: Challenges for comprehensive planning. Journal of Environmental Planning and Management, 46(5), 733-754.

Godschalk, D. R., et al. (2009). Estimating the value of foresight: aggregate analysis of natural hazard mitigation benefits and costs. Journal of Environmental Planning and Management, 52(6), 739-756.

Gurley, K., & Masters, F. (2011). Post-2004 hurricane field survey of residential building performance. Natural Hazards Review, 12(4), 177-183.

Gurley, K., et al. (2006). Post 2004 Hurricane Field Survey of Residential Building Performance. Natural Hazards Review, 7(2), 29-44.

Haasnoot, M., et al. (2013). Dynamic adaptive policy pathways: A method for crafting robust decisions for a deeply uncertain world. Global Environmental Change, 23(2), 485-498.

Hebert, P. J., et al. (1997). The deadliest, costliest, and most intense United States hurricanes of this century (and other frequently requested hurricane facts). NOAA Technical Memorandum NWS TPC-1.

Highfield, W. E., et al. (2014). Mitigation planning: Why hazard exposure, structural vulnerability, and social vulnerability matter. Journal of Planning Education and Research, 34(3), 287-300.

Holmes, J. D. (2015). Wind Loading of Structures (3rd ed.). CRC Press.

Insurance Information Institute. (2022). Florida's Property Insurance Market: Spiraling Towards Collapse.

Insurance Institute for Business & Home Safety. (2007). Hurricane Wilma: Nature's Window into Florida's Wind Insurance Problem. IBHS.

Insurance Institute for Business & Home Safety. (2015). Hurricane Charley: Lessons Learned in Building Performance. IBHS.

Insurance Institute for Business & Home Safety. (2020). FORTIFIED Home™ Hurricane Standards. IBHS.

Insurance Institute for Business & Home Safety. (2020). Rating the States: 2020 Update.

Insurance Institute for Business & Home Safety. (2021). FORTIFIED in Your State: North Carolina. IBHS.

International Code Council. (2021). Code Adoption Map.

Intergovernmental Panel on Climate Change. (2022). Climate Change 2022: Impacts, Adaptation and Vulnerability.

IPCC. (2021). Climate Change 2021: The Physical Science Basis. Contribution of Working Group I to the Sixth Assessment Report of the Intergovernmental Panel on Climate Change.

Kang, G. S., et al. (2009). Life-cycle cost analysis of high-performance residential buildings with focus on energy efficiency. Advances in Building Energy Research, 3(1), 163-188.

Kareem, A., & Kijewski, T. (2002). Mitigation of motions of tall buildings with specific examples of recent applications. Wind and Structures, 5(2-4), 273-298.

Keenan, J. M. (2018). Climate adaptation finance and investment in California. Routledge.

Kiliccote, S., et al. (2014). Smart buildings and demand response. In Smart Grid Communications and Networking (pp. 273-302). Cambridge University Press.

Kirkpatrick, H., & Smith, L. C. (2011). Response to "Property Assessed Clean Energy (PACE) Financing: Update on Commercial Programs". Clinton Climate Initiative, 3.

Klotzbach, P. J., et al. (2018). Continental U.S. Hurricane Landfall Frequency and Associated Damage: Observations and Future Risks. Bulletin of the American Meteorological Society, 99(7), 1359-1376.

Knowles, S. G., & Kunreuther, H. C. (2014). Troubled waters: The National Flood Insurance Program in historical perspective. Journal of Policy History, 26(3), 327-353.

Knutson, T., et al. (2020). Tropical cyclones and climate change assessment: Part II: Projected response to anthropogenic warming. Bulletin of the American Meteorological Society, 101(3), E303-E322.

Knutson, T. R., et al. (2010). Tropical cyclones and climate change. Nature Geoscience, 3(3), 157-163.

Kossin, J. P. (2018). A global slowdown of tropical-cyclone translation speed. Nature, 558(7708), 104-107.

Kunreuther, H. (2006). Disaster mitigation and insurance: Learning from Katrina. The Annals of the American Academy of Political and Social Science, 604(1), 208-227.

Kunreuther, H. C., & Michel-Kerjan, E. O. (2009). At war with the weather: Managing large-scale risks in a new era of catastrophes. MIT Press.

Kwasinski, A., et al. (2009). Performance of electric power systems in the 2008 Hurricane Ike disaster. In IEEE Systems Conference, 2009, 253-258.

Landsea, C. W., et al. (2004). The Atlantic hurricane database re-analysis project: Documentation for the 1851-1910 alterations and additions to the HURDAT database. Hurricanes and Typhoons: Past, Present and Future, 177-221.

Li, Y., & Ellingwood, B. R. (2006). Hurricane damage to residential construction in the US: Importance of uncertainty modeling in risk assessment. Engineering Structures, 28(7), 1009-1018.

Lin, N., et al. (2010). Risk assessment of hurricane wind and rainfall hazards for New York City. Natural Hazards Review, 11(2), 49-56.

Lstiburek, J. (2006). Water management guide. Building Science Press.

May, P. J. (1997). State regulatory roles: Choices in the regulation of building safety. State & Local Government Review, 29(2), 70-80.

May, P. J. (2003). Performance-based regulation and regulatory regimes: The saga of leaky buildings. Law & Policy, 25(4), 381-401.

May, P. J. (2007). Regulatory regimes and accountability. Regulation & Governance, 1(1), 8-26.

May, P. J., & Koski, C. (2013). Addressing public risks: Extreme events and critical infrastructures. Review of Policy Research, 30(2), 139-159.

Meacham, B. J. (2010). Performance-based building regulatory systems: principles and experiences. Inter-jurisdictional Regulatory Collaboration Committee.

Meecham, D., et al. (1991). Wind loads on buildings with steep roofs. Journal of Wind Engineering and Industrial Aerodynamics, 38(2-3), 257-272.

Mehta, K. C., et al. (1992). Wind speed-damage correlation in Hurricane Frederic. Journal of Structural Engineering, 118(2), 342-355.

Minor, J. E. (1994). Windborne debris and the building envelope. Journal of Wind Engineering and Industrial Aerodynamics, 53(1-2), 207-227.

Moser, S. C., & Ekstrom, J. A. (2010). A framework to diagnose barriers to climate change adaptation. Proceedings of the National Academy of Sciences, 107(51), 22026-22031.

Mostafavi, N., & Inman, D. (2018). Improving the resilience of structures using adaptive building envelopes. Engineering Structures, 175, 876-888.

Mykle, R. (2002). Killer 'Cane: The Deadly Hurricane of 1935. Cooper Square Press.

Nadal, N. C., et al. (2010). Building damage caused by flooding: The Xynthia case study. Journal of Performance of Constructed Facilities, 24(4), 371-378.

National Hurricane Center. (2005). Tropical Cyclone Report: Hurricane Jeanne. NOAA.

National Hurricane Center. (2022). Tropical Cyclone Climatology.

National Institute of Building Sciences. (2019). Natural Hazard Mitigation Saves: 2019 Report.

National Research Council. (2014). Reducing Coastal Risk on the East and Gulf Coasts. The National Academies Press.

Nicholls, R. J., & Cazenave, A. (2010). Sea-level rise and its impact on coastal zones. Science, 328(5985), 1517-1520.

NOAA Office for Coastal Management. (2021). Fast Facts: Hurricane Costs.

North Carolina Building Code Council. (2018). North Carolina State Building Code: Residential Code Cost Analysis.

North Carolina Department of Insurance. (2019). Insurance Premium Discounts for FORTIFIED Homes. NC DOI.

Pacheco-Torgal, F., & Jalali, S. (2011). Nanotechnology: Advantages and drawbacks in the field of construction and building materials. Construction and Building Materials, 25(2), 582-590.

Pacheco-Torgal, F., & Labrincha, J. A. (2013). The future of construction materials research and the seventh UN Millennium Development Goal: A few insights. Construction and Building Materials, 40, 729-737.

Pan, M., et al. (2018). A framework of indicators for assessing construction automation and robotics in the sustainability context. Journal of Cleaner Production, 182, 82-95.

Peacock, W. G. (2003). Hurricane mitigation status and factors influencing mitigation status among Florida's single-family homeowners. Natural Hazards Review, 4(3), 149-158.

Peacock, W. G., et al. (2005). Hurricane risk perceptions among Florida's single-family homeowners. Landscape and Urban Planning, 73(2-3), 120-135.

Peacock, W. G., et al. (2018). The adoption and implementation of hazard-resistant building codes. Natural Hazards Review, 19(4), 04018018.

Peek, L., et al. (2020). Natural hazards science: Innovations in DRR research and practice. Natural Hazards Review, 21(2), 04020012.

Pinelli, J. P., et al. (2004). Hurricane damage prediction model for residential structures. Journal of Structural Engineering, 130(11), 1685-1691.

Prevatt, D. O., et al. (2012). Making the case for improved structural design: Tornado outbreaks of 2011. Leadership and Management in Engineering, 12(4), 254-270.

Prevatt, D. O., et al. (2019). Investigation of Optional Enhanced Construction Techniques for the Wind, Flood, and Storm Surge Provisions of the Florida Building Code. University of Florida Engineering School of Sustainable Infrastructure and Environment.

Rappaport, E. N. (1993). Preliminary report: Hurricane Andrew, 16-28 August 1992. National Hurricane Center.

Robertson, I. N., et al. (2007). Cyclic testing of hurricane ties for coastal construction. Journal of Architectural Engineering, 13(1), 9-19.

Roos, P. J., et al. (2003). Wave-induced forces on vertical structures in flooding conditions. Coastal Engineering, 47(4), 367-388.

Rose, A., et al. (2007). Benefit-cost analysis of FEMA hazard mitigation grants. Natural Hazards Review, 8(4), 97-111.

Sailor, D. J. (2014). Risks of summertime extreme thermal conditions in buildings as a result of climate change and exacerbation of urban heat islands. Building and Environment, 78, 81-88.

Schwerdt, R. W., et al. (1979). Meteorological criteria for standard project hurricane and probable maximum hurricane windfields, Gulf and East Coasts of the United States. NOAA Technical Report NWS 23.

Shanmugam, B., et al. (2009). Hurricane loss estimation models: Opportunities for improving the state of the art. Bulletin of the American Meteorological Society, 90(12), 1833-1842.

Simiu, E., & Scanlan, R. H. (1996). Wind Effects on Structures: Fundamentals and Applications to Design (3rd ed.). John Wiley & Sons.

Simmons, K. M., & Czajkowski, J. (2018). Framing the Policy Debate Over Building Codes in Hurricane-Prone States. Coastal Management, 46(3), 298-314.

Simmons, K. M., & Sutter, D. (2007). Tornado shelters and the manufactured home parks market. Natural Hazards, 43(3), 365-378.

Simmons, K. M., et al. (2015). Developing coastal wind speed maps for building design: A case study. Journal of Wind Engineering and Industrial Aerodynamics, 146, 76-83.

Simmons, K. M., et al. (2018). Economic effectiveness of implementing a statewide building code: The case of Florida. Land Economics, 94(2), 155-174.

Simmons, K. M., et al. (2019). Effectiveness of a FORTIFIED Home™ Hurricane Standard. Weather, Climate, and Society, 11(4), 917-927.

Sparks, P. R., et al. (1994). Wind damage to envelopes of houses and consequent insurance losses. Journal of Wind Engineering and Industrial Aerodynamics, 53(1-2), 145-155.

Stathopoulos, T. (1984). Wind loads on low-rise buildings: a review of the state of the art. Engineering Structures, 6(2), 119-135.

Suaris, W., & Khan, M. S. (1995). Residential construction failures caused by Hurricane Andrew. Journal of Performance of Constructed Facilities, 9(1), 10-15.

Sweet, W. V., et al. (2022). Global and Regional Sea Level Rise Scenarios for the United States: Updated Mean Projections and Extreme Water Level Probabilities Along U.S. Coastlines. NOAA Technical Report NOS CO-OPS 092.

Talen, E. (2013). Zoning For and Against Sprawl: The Case for Form-Based Codes. Journal of Urban Design, 18(2), 175-200.

Tam, V. W., et al. (2007). Towards adoption of prefabrication in construction. Building and Environment, 42(10), 3642-3654.

Texas Department of Insurance. (2019). Windstorm Resistant Construction Cost Analysis.

Trenberth, K. E., et al. (2018). Hurricane Harvey links to ocean heat content and climate change adaptation. Earth's Future, 6(5), 730-744.

Tsikoudakis, M. (2018). Construction innovation targets severe weather resilience. Business Insurance, 52(5), 20-21.

Twisdale, L. A., et al. (1996). Analysis of hurricane windborne debris impact risk for residential structures. Journal of Wind Engineering and Industrial Aerodynamics, 60, 345-358.

van de Lindt, J. W., & Dao, T. N. (2009). Performance-based wind engineering for wood-frame buildings. Journal of Structural Engineering, 135(2), 169-177.

van de Lindt, J. W., et al. (2007). Performance-based engineering of wood frame housing: Fragility analysis methodology and case studies. Journal of Structural Engineering, 133(9), 1290-1299.

Vamvatsikos, D., & Cornell, C. A. (2002). Incremental dynamic analysis. Earthquake Engineering & Structural Dynamics, 31(3), 491-514.

Vickery, P. J., et al. (2009). U.S. hurricane wind speed risk and uncertainty. Journal of Structural Engineering, 135(3), 301-320.

Westerink, J. J., et al. (2008). A basin-to channel-scale unstructured grid hurricane storm surge model applied to southern Louisiana. Monthly Weather Review, 136(3), 833-864.

Will, L. E. (1978). Okeechobee Hurricane: Killer Storms in the Everglades. Great Outdoors Publishing Company.

Wilson, A. (2006). Passive survivability: A new design criterion for buildings. Environmental Building News, 15(5), 1-8.

Zevenbergen, C., et al. (2018). Adaptive delta management: a comparison between the Netherlands and Bangladesh Delta Program. International Journal of River Basin Management, 16(3), 299-305.

This comprehensive reference list includes all the unique sources cited throughout the book, providing a robust foundation for the research and analysis presented in the document. It demonstrates the wide range of academic, governmental, and industry sources consulted, enhancing the credibility and thoroughness of the book.

Appendix B

Glossary of Technical Terms

Adaptive Management: An approach to decision-making that involves adjusting policies or practices based on observed outcomes and new information.

Aerodynamic Design: Building design that minimizes wind resistance and reduces wind-induced forces on structures.

Base Flood Elevation (BFE): The elevation of surface water resulting from a flood that has a 1% chance of occurring in any given year.

Benefit-Cost Ratio: A metric used in cost-benefit analysis, calculated by dividing the total benefits of a project by its total costs.

Building Envelope: The physical separator between the interior and exterior of a building, including walls, roof, windows, and doors.

Code Plus: Enhanced building standards that exceed minimum code requirements, specifically designed to improve hurricane resistance.

Continuous Load Path: An engineered method of connecting all parts of a building, from roof to foundation, to resist wind forces.

Ductility: The ability of a material or structure to deform plastically under stress without fracturing.

Dynamic Facade Systems: Building envelope components that can adapt to changing environmental conditions, potentially enhancing hurricane resistance.

Freeboard: Additional height above the Base Flood Elevation, providing an extra margin of safety against flooding.

High-Performance Concrete: Specialized concrete mixtures designed for enhanced strength, durability, or other specific performance characteristics.

Hurricane Straps: Metal connectors used to secure roof trusses or rafters to the top of walls, enhancing wind resistance.

Hydrostatic Pressure: The pressure exerted by a fluid at equilibrium due to the force of gravity, relevant in flood-resistant design.

Hydrodynamic Forces: Forces exerted by moving water, such as those experienced during storm surge or flooding events.

Impact-Resistant Glazing: Windows and doors designed to withstand impacts from wind-borne debris during hurricanes.

Mitigation: Actions taken to reduce long-term risk to people and property from hazards.

Net Present Value (NPV): The difference between the present value of cash inflows and the present value of cash outflows over a period of time, used in capital budgeting to analyze the profitability of an investment or project.

Passive Survivability: A building's ability to maintain critical life-support conditions if utilities are lost for an extended period.

Performance-Based Design: An approach to building design that focuses on achieving specific performance objectives rather than prescribing specific methods.

Resilience: The ability of a system, community, or society exposed to hazards to resist, absorb, accommodate, and recover from the effects of a hazard.

Ring-Shank Nails: Nails with circular ridges on the shank, providing greater withdrawal resistance compared to smooth-shank nails.

Risk-Informed Regulations: Building codes or standards that consider both the likelihood and potential consequences of different hazard scenarios.

Secondary Water Barrier: An additional layer of protection against water intrusion, often installed beneath the primary roof covering.

Self-Healing Materials: Innovative materials capable of automatically repairing small cracks or damage without external intervention.

Shear Walls: Structural elements designed to resist lateral forces parallel to the plane of the wall.

Smart Building Technologies: Advanced systems that monitor and control various building functions, potentially enhancing hurricane resilience.

Storm Surge: An abnormal rise in sea level accompanying a hurricane or other intense storm, potentially causing severe coastal flooding.

Structural Health Monitoring: The process of implementing a damage detection and characterization strategy for engineering structures.

Ultra-High-Performance Concrete (UHPC): A specialized concrete mixture with exceptional strength and durability characteristics.

Uplift Forces: Upward forces exerted on building components, particularly roofs, by wind during hurricanes.

Wind Load: The force exerted on a structure by wind, typically measured in pounds per square foot.

Wind-Borne Debris: Objects picked up and carried by strong winds during a hurricane, potentially causing significant damage to structures.

About the Author

Don D. Brown is a respected author, consultant, and former legislator with a distinguished career in public policy and insurance reform. A retired insurance agent from DeFuniak Springs, Florida, Brown served on the Walton County Commission, as Republican State Committeeman, Chairman of the Walton County Republican Executive Committee, and as a State Representative in the Florida House of Representatives.

During his eight years in the legislature, Brown became one of Florida's most informed and outspoken voices on insurance and financial issues. Twice recognized by both the Florida Association of Insurance Agents and the Florida Association of Insurance and Financial Advisors, he was known for advocating market-based solutions, smaller government, and principle-driven policymaking. In 2007, he stood nearly alone in opposing HB1A, a massive expansion of government into private insurance markets—objections that time has largely validated.

Brown is the author of numerous books and white papers exploring the intersection of insurance, economics, and public policy, including:

Books

1. *Drowning in Denial: Behavioral Economics and Coastal Insurance Markets: A Path to Resilience* (2024)
2. *Fortifying the Future: Code Plus Standards for Hurricane Resilience and Economic Stability* (2024)

3. *The High Cost of Hidden Risk: Why Florida's Insurance Crisis Can't Be Fixed Without Facing Reality* (2024)

4. *The Capital Drain: How Policy Uncertainty Weakens Catastrophe Insurance Markets* (2024)

5. *Beyond Indemnity: The Evolution, Complexity, and Future of Homeowners Insurance* (2024)

6. *Navigating Uncertainty in Florida's Property Insurance Market: A Strategic Framework for Resilience* (2024)

7. *The 9 Guideline Principles to Enact Change: A Legislator's Memoir — From Outhouse to State House* (2021)

8. *From Roots to Realization: A Journey from the Outhouse to the Statehouse* (2021)

9. *From Roots to Realization: A Legislative Journey* (2021)

10. *Essays on Insurance and Public Policy* (2021)

White Papers

1. *The Importance of Guiding Principles in Public Policymaking*

2. *How Do Other Jurisdictions Manage Hurricane Risk Exposure?*

3. *Parametric Insurance Claims Processing and Smart Contracts on the Blockchain*

4. *Florida's Homeowners Insurance Crisis: A Root Cause Approach with Guiding Principles*

5. *9 Guiding Principles and the "However" Response*

6. *Solving Florida's Homeowners Insurance Crisis: A Strategic Root Cause Analysis* (with Dennis Ross)

7. *Nine Guiding Principles to Enact Change: A Legislator's Journey from Outhouse to Statehouse* (comparative study)

8. *Beyond the Beach Brochure: A Comprehensive Analysis of Florida's Homeowner Insurance Crisis*

Brown continues to write and speak extensively on resilience, insurance markets, and the role of principled policymaking in addressing complex challenges.

Contact Information:

Don D. Brown
PO Box 866
DeFuniak Springs, FL 32435
info@donanddiane.com
www. dondbrown.live

A Note to Readers

Thank you for reading *Fortifying the Future: Code Plus Standards for Hurricane Resilience and Economic Stability.* Books like this reach further and influence more lives when readers like you take a few moments to share your thoughts.

If you found this book informative, thought-provoking, or valuable in your professional or personal life, I would be deeply grateful if you would post a brief review. Reviews not only help other readers discover the book but also encourage ongoing conversations about resilience, insurance reform, and building stronger communities.

Your voice matters. Please consider leaving a review on Amazon, Goodreads, or any platform where you share books with others. Even a few sentences can make a lasting difference.

With gratitude,

Don D. Brown

Made in the USA
Monee, IL
14 November 2025

34678661R00144